Beyond Th
Book 1:

Communications with the Co-Creators

by
Guy Steven Needler

OZARK
MOUNTAIN
PUBLISHING

PO Box 754, Huntsville, AR 72740
800-935-0045 or 479-738-2348; fax 479-738-2448
www.ozarkmt.com

For permission, serialization, condensation, adaptions, or for our catalog of other publications, write to Ozark Mountain Publishing, Inc., P.O. box 754, Huntsville, AR 72740, ATTN: Permissions Department.

Library of Congress Cataloging-in-Publication Data

Needler, Guy, 1961-
  Beyond the Source – Book 1; Communications with the Co-Creators, by Guy Steven Needler
Dialogues through meditation with the first 6 of the twelve Co-Creators that operate outside of our own Source Entitiy.

1. Source Entities 2. Co-Creators 3. Origin 4. Metaphysics
I. Needler, Guy, 1961- II. Co-Creators III. Metaphysics IV. Title

Library of Congress Catalog Card Number: 2012938630

ISBN: 978-1-886940-33-8

Cover Art and Layout: www.noir33.com
Book set in: Times New Roman
Book Design: Julia Degan

Published by:

OZARK
MOUNTAIN
PUBLISHING

WWW.OZARKMT.COM
Printed in the United States of America

Table of Contents

Introduction

The Origin's Creation of Twelve Source Entities

If you have read *The History of God, a story of the beginning of everything,* which gave the reader an insight into how I started my higher level communications and managed to communicate with spiritual/energetic entities whilst gaining insights into the wonders that are all around us and the truth about our legends and myths, then you will remember that there were twelve Source Entities created by the Origin. The first one being discussed in some limited detail in the book above was our very own Source Entity (SE), whom we refer to as God, the being that created our universe. In reality the Origin should really be considered as God as it created the Source Entities, but I think that the Origin is well beyond the need for this sort of primitive nomenclature, which is only necessary for us humans in our low level of physically trapped conscious existence.

It was during the countless days editing and compiling the channeled texts for the book above that I realized that in order to keep the records straight, I would need to set up communications with each of these other entities in turn in order to gain a basic understanding of the details of the work that they have done in their own environments, which I expected to differ from one another.

As a result of the potential level of difference, I was held in a certain level of trepidation. For instance, would I be able to understand what was being channeled through me? And would it be in a format that could be understood by those who wish to learn the knowledge that could well be totally over all of our heads? Upon reflection, I decided that I had been "here" before and should not try to predict what would come.

Welcome back!

Chapter 1

Source Entity One—
The Master of Our Multiverse

[For those who haven't read *The History of God: a story of the beginning of everything*, SE is Source Entity, and ME is Guy Needler, the author of this book.]

SE: Well, that was a rather grand entrance you wrote on the first page.

ME: *I would hardly call it a grand entrance, more of a preamble, a "getting the audience warmed up" for the* The Shape of Things to Come.

SE: You can quote HG Wells if you want, but we need to get down to the real business of letting your readers know what is happening in the wider areas of the Origin, what my peers are up to, and what they are accomplishing, not writing science fiction. Although what you are about to experience over the next months of communication may get you wondering on these lines.

One thing is certain—this is not a task to be taken lightly. Indeed, it is one that you WILL struggle with, specifically with the concepts that some of the Source Entities will present to you. It is with this thought about your struggling that I offer you this opportunity for help. Before we delve into the old ground of my creation, some of which I have no doubt you will cut and paste from the other texts and some of which will be new information, I suggest that I act as your guide, mentor, and main point of contact when establishing contact and ultimately

1

communicating with the other Source Entities, especially as you will need to meet them in their own environments. Therefore, I will be your passport to the other Source environments whilst delivering this book.

ME: Why do I need your help—not that I am refusing it? I can communicate with the Origin all on my own, so why not them?

SE: They are not as capable of understanding the entities that are created outside their environments as the Origin and I are. The Origin is the source of everything; I am the Source of you and your environment, so we both have no problem tuning in to your frequencies and level of communication whilst in the physical. Some of the Sources don't go anywhere nearly as low as ten frequency levels above you—let alone down to your level—so they are bound to have problems communicating with you directly, hence my insistence in offering help in this matter.

ME: Thank you. Now I understand. I feel quite excited about meeting these other Source Entities.

SE: And so you should, for you go where no man has gone before.

ME: No one!

SE: What?

ME: No one, Gene Roddenberry's original introductory text was changed to say NO ONE, not NO MAN.

SE: One, this is no time for Star Trek jokes and two, you are not NO ONE. You are a man, currently, and NO MAN to date has done what you are about to do.

ME: Touché.

SE: Now let's get on with it. Let's get down to the nitty gritty.

The Source Entity Becomes Aware of Its Self and Its Environment

ME: I guess at this point I will be doing some copying from the first book?

SE: Only where it is relevant. There will be some correlation, but don't forget that in the first set of dialogues I was talking about what we (the twelve Source Entities) were doing collectively and not individually. There is no point in going over old ground, such as how I/we developed the physical side of the human race, for that would not be good value in terms of reading time and text space. However, I will reiterate what is essential and, therefore, needs to be fleshed out more.

ME: O.K., let's start from the beginning then and deal with the "detail" as we get to it. What happened at the start of your existence?

SE: In the beginning it was like I was part of the Origin but still the Origin—not as I am now. It was like I was one thought of what was going on in the Origin's consciousness—one thought that was given substance, time to be, individual space to move around in, but still a thought nevertheless. I knew I was the Origin and was separate from the Origin all at the same time. It was as if my individual awareness was like a memory that is in the front of your mind for a moment, and then is gone, only to reappear later when you give it enough attention or when you are not trying too hard to remember. It's just like when you remember a memory that you hold in your mind fleetingly but then lose, resulting in a struggle to recover the memory. It is this enhanced attention to the fleeting awareness that I had lost that later gave rise to the ability to hold the level of awareness for long enough to bring it into the consciousness state again. At first it was hard, and I have no doubt that many, many millennia

3

passed before I had reached full independent consciousness.

ME: So what was the defining moment of consciousness for you? When did you realize that you were truly individual but were still part of a bigger entity, the Origin?

SE: Actually, it was not so much of a defining moment, more like a defining conversation.

ME: A conversation? You mean you were told by the Origin you were an individual entity?

SE: In a nutshell, yes. We all were, but this conversation only took place when each of us had achieved a critical level of awareness and, therefore, consciousness. As I stated in the first dialogue we had, one of us is still in this "dawning" state of awareness. You will experience this when we need to enter its environment.

You see, the Origin was watching our development at all times and chose the moment for communication and education when it knew it would be at its most effective.

ME: The Origin educated you as well?

SE: Only to the point of what I was brought into existence for and what the rules of being in existence were. Some of these I have passed on to all of you, for they are relevant to all entities that are "of the Origin."

ME: Let's go back to that moment of defining moment of consciousness.

SE: The moment was just before the Origin contacted me to advise me on why I was created. I had noticed that I was aware of my own "self" almost continuously and could remember what I needed to do to maintain consciousness. I could also remember what I had done before although I had not yet understood that I could access what I would do next. In essence, I only knew the past and the present; I could not access the future. In some respects I was just like you are in your incarnate state right now. Another defining moment before the Origin contacted me was the recognition of other entities, eleven of them, all in a similar level of conscious awareness as me. Of course, some were more aware, others were less aware, but on average we were much the same. The clincher here was the ability to communicate with the other Source Entities, which to all intent and purposes, just happened.

ME: *What?! You all developed a common language all at the same time?*

SE: No, no. We contacted each other energetically—each of us understanding the other without the need to learn a language. I was later to learn from the Origin that basic energetic communication was one of the things that had been given to us during our creation. This communication medium being based upon the Origin's thought process.

ME: *So what did the Origin say to you?*

SE: First, the Origin spoke to each of us individually, not all at once, for we were not all ready to be advised on our roles. Second, each of us had to have established enough awareness and consciousness to be able to realize and understand that we were part of a larger—much larger— entity and that we were parts of this much larger entity given individuality.

ME: *How did you understand that you were part of the Origin?*

SE: Simply by noticing that I could hear the thoughts of the Origin. These thoughts were the thoughts of an entity in deep contemplation.

ME: *Not by traveling to the edge of the Origin's boundary?*

SE: The Origin has no boundary as you know it, so this would not have provided the evidence for being a component of the Origin. Once I established that the thoughts were not coming from the others—the other eleven Source Entities—I drew the conclusion that I must be part of something bigger. I reached out in communication to the Origin, and it responded. From that point onward, I was in constant communication with the Origin, learning the reasons for my existence and what task I had to undertake to explore the self and the Origin and improve my awareness—in essence, evolve.

ME: Did you have any choice in the matter of the task at hand?

SE: There was no choice for the task was the very reason for my existence.

ME: What rules did you have?

SE: None.

ME: What time frame do you have to work to?

SE: None.

The only remit was to explore, learn, become more aware, and evolve. In doing so, the Origin said that it would also evolve, and it would do this by experiencing all that I experienced at that same time as I experienced it. It said that it was doing this many times all at the same time, for its thirst for expanding its own awareness of self was insatiable.

ME: And it's still doing it now?

SE: Yes, it's still doing it now after many, many billions of years. This is the only way I can relay to you the amount of attention it has dedicated to the subject of knowing itself better, becoming more aware, and evolving.

ME: Let's get back to the subject of you becoming aware. I can relate to becoming aware from the point of view of a child, as I once was.

SE: As you have been many times.

ME: Yes, but I never realized that I was aware of self until I was—I have to think hard about at what point this occurred—sometime in the early pre-teenage years. And this was only because of being ridiculed at school for having such way-out ideas, ones which I now realize were manifested from my ability to tap into the higher frequencies and, therefore, the greater reality—which now allows me to communicate with you and the Origin and other entities, such as Byron.

When I was a child, I just was me. I had no real feeling of individual awareness. I just did what children do but with no realization of self although I was aware that I was different somehow, apart from the others. This was a feeling that I found was quite strange, for I always thought that I was part of something important. As a result, I always found it hard to be "part of the gang," so to speak, and they considered me as a bit strange.

So you realized that you were you at the point just before the Origin communicated with you and a little after the time you noticed that there where eleven others?

SE: Yes, I became aware that I was able to experience different things by changing the location of myself. By location I do not mean spatial as you are thinking but both dimensional and frequential. When I moved myself into different "locations," I experienced different things happening to my energies, my "self." These were predominantly sensations on many levels—many more levels than you can possibly imagine. It was during one of these sensation experiencing moments that I recognized my "self" as being individual. I was fully aware of cause and effect. If I did one thing, something else would happen. If I did something different, then this was rewarded with a different effect.

The awareness of self is the most important milestone on any entity's road to evolution. Further, the awareness of awareness is the milestone in an entity's road to evolution where the veil of illusion is lifted to reveal the true reality of existence. This is the point where everything is made clear. Nothing is misunderstood. There is no environmental limitation, there is no limitation in understanding, there is no limitation in capacity for learning, and, therefore, no limitation in the ability to evolve. There is only opportunity.

ME: *So apart from the feeling of cause and effect, what else gave you the nudge you needed to become aware?*

SE: Nothing else, only the experience of cause and effect and the recognition of the other eleven Source Entities. Although at this point, none of us recognized what we were fully capable of as we were not yet in receipt of our instructions from the Origin. Let me say here though that the element of cause and effect as a factor of recognizing self-awareness should not be played down, for it is the recognition of an individual's ability to create that is the deciding factor. Cause creates effect, and to cause an effect that is the manifestation of pure creativity is to create the feeling of satisfaction; with satisfaction comes recognition of self and awareness of self in the environment of existence.

ME: *So what you are saying is that you really got to grips with recognizing your "self" when you were creating.*

SE: Eloquently put. Creativity is one of the most important things that an entity can do; it is a reflection of self and is, therefore, the doorway to self-realization, awareness. Many of your artists, engineers, scientists, and authors create, and it is with their creations that they realize who and what they are—their creations are an extension of their *"selves"* with their creations, therefore, acting as mirrors, making recognition easier.

ME: *I get the feeling that pride has a hand in this as well.*

SE: To some extent, but pride is only a feeling of well-being, of ego. However, as ego is the prerequisite for the state of *"I am,"* it also helps in being one of the markers on the road to awareness.

Creativity is the ultimate marker. It is the result of action on behalf of the individual. It is the debris left behind to indicate existence, and it is the evidence needed by the individual entity to make the jump from mere existence to the realization of existence. It was, therefore, when I created different things by manipulating and changing the natural representation of the energy surrounding me that I made the connection between mere existence and realization of self.

ME: *If I remember correctly, then this must have been around the time that you were creating myriad patterns and shapes—what we now recognize as galaxies and planets.*

SE: Well remembered, but not correct as the galaxies and planets were not that which currently exist in your universal environment.

ME: *You mean that you wiped them out? You started again?*

SE: Yes, it was merely a game. Nothing was lost, and everything was gained. My awareness was gained. Don't forget that creativity is a reflection of self, and in this instance, the shapes and patterns caused me to reflect inwardly and recognize achievement. As previously stated, the achievement of creativity is a reflection of self creating recognition of self and, therefore, granting the individual entity the gift of awareness. I subsequently became aware and was contacted by the Origin moments later, which further confirmed my awareness.

ME: *So would you completely wipe out the universes that you have currently, the ones that humanity and the rest of your entities exist within?*

SE: I could and I might at some point in the future, but one thing that I will not do is remove the energy-based entities that I have created. These would stay and populate the new environment. Actually, I see no need to recreate a new environment, as there is much to gain from the current one.

ME: *Why would you keep the entities from this set of universes if you decided to start again and not wipe them out as well?*

SE: Simple. The reason for keeping the entities that I have created in this universe is because they are part of me, and I am part of them. If I consolidated back into oneness all

9

that I have created and given individuality to, I would lose myriad opportunities to experience the vast number of experiences in the multipolous [multiple of multiple of multiple] ways that I am now. Moreover, I would lose the continued level of evolutionary experience. Experience and evolution takes time to accomplish as does the ability to understand how to evolve in the most effective way. All this would be lost and have to be re-learnt by the new entities that I would need to create. No, I see no need to do this; it would not be beneficial to me as it would ultimately slow down my speed of evolution.

Creation of the Universes

ME: We have discussed your awakening and awareness of your "self" in brief and the fact that you became more aware of self when the Origin communicated to you and the other Source Entities it created.

SE: Yes, we have.

ME: I would like to know more about what the Origin said to you all and what made you decide on the format of entities and multiversal environment you chose.

SE: As I said in our previous dialogues, the other Source Entities and I were having a whale of a time. We were allowed to do anything we wanted.

ME: Was this your own choice?

SE: No. The first thing that the Origin said to us when we were aware of each other and the Origin was that we had to learn the art of experience—literally, how to experience and learn/evolve from those experiences. The time in between our being aware of *"self,"* each other, and the Origin was next to no time at all. It was almost instantaneous from my perspective, but you may think that millennia had gone by if you had to measure the time in human terms. At this point the Origin made us aware of its intentions for us and educated us on the reasons for our existence and the task that it was going to set us—all of which would result in the Origin's accelerated evolution and experience of its *"self."*

The first thing we had to do was just create. We were told to create and experience anything and everything in any way we felt we would benefit by, simply by experiencing what we had created. This was primarily energetic at first but ultimately deviated into the frequential and dimensional aspects of creativity.

ME: *How do you mean?*

SE: Well, I think I had better focus on my own experience now as I am aware that I could start to explain what we were all experiencing rather than just myself. This will come out separately with each of the dialogues we have with the other Source Entities.

ME: *That's fine by me.*

SE: Let us continue then. Once I had experienced creativity from the energetic aspect in a general environmental sense, i.e., who and where I was, I started to realize that the same level of creativity was not represented in the same way the higher up or lower down the frequencies. This changed significantly as I introduced the dimensional aspect to the object or item that I was creating. I noticed that if I created something in my current general environment, the representation in the higher and lower frequencies/dimensions was not the same. In fact, the change was quite marked.

ME: *Give me an example.*

SE: Let me take something that you would relate to as an example then, galaxies. When I created something that had singularity and was manifest into a lower frequency, it gained form. The lower down the frequencies I went, the more substantial the form was. When I went up the frequencies, the more insubstantial the form was and the more, for the want of a better word, fluidic it became.

ME: *You mean it became a fluid?*

SE: No, it is a figure of speech. By fluidic I mean that it was more without form. What's more it was able to interject in between the dimensions the higher up the frequencies it was. For example, it was so formless it had the ability to exist in any environment. Similarly, the lower down the frequencies, the more form the creation had and the less able it was to interject between the dimensions and lower frequencies. In fact, it ended up being locked into one set of frequencies and a corresponding dimension as well. The *"formless"* was purely energetic; the *"formed"* became nebulae in some of the higher frequencies, suns in the lower frequencies, and planets in the lowest frequencies. What was interesting is that what you call galaxies are not specifically *"form"* as the level of form is local to the frequencies that the *"formed"* naturally migrated to or were attracted to. This meant that as I created things that had form, they were either more or less in substance and had more or less form due to the pockets of higher or lower frequencies, i.e., what I created was not pure of frequency or dimension. This explains why galaxies are what they are—vast areas of space with local areas of density—the local areas of density correlating to the lower frequencies, therefore, creating *"form."* That which was *"formed"* resulted in the round objects you call suns and planets.

I found this fascinating and was entirely motivated into understanding that part that I had created that was form rather than formless. Hence, the universe you have today.

ME: *So you messed around with energy to create what we now recognize as galaxies.*

SE: That's about the size of it.

ME: So when did you decide to stop with the set of galaxies that we have today, bearing in mind that we also now recognize that there are myriad universes as well, each having its own set of galaxies? So here's a second question as well. When did you decide to stop with the set of universes that we have today?

SE: Essentially when I realized that I was re-creating for the sake of it, I realized that I was not giving the creations that I had made enough time to mature and become something on their own. Everything that I had created was being manipulated by me just to see what it would look like. I had not recognized the possibility of extended creation through observation of form changing on its own as a result of its own inertia.

ME: What does extended creation mean?

SE: It means the creation of new creativity by that that has been created. In essence, that is what you, mankind, are doing now.

Creation being created by that which was created—this was truly fascinating. Why I stopped re-creating the galaxies, which by the way are a function of creating universes, was because I realized that the level of creation resulting from me doing nothing but observing, observing that which I had created, was something significantly more interesting than I had even considered as a possibility. It was fun, but more importantly, it was a window into a new dimension of evolution for me. The universes were the environment from which the creation of physical form, the galaxies, suns and planets would ultimately take on their own dynamics. I, therefore, stopped the creation, re-creation cycle when I saw a pattern of creativity emerge that I thought had the most potential, i.e., one that would bear the most fruit with the minimum of interaction.

ME: So how did you create the universes?

SE: The big bang theory that your scientists propose as the start of the universe is so far away from the truth it is not even worth considering. I didn't create the universes by igniting a gigantic match and it exploding and expanding, although it does sound like a good idea. No, I created the universes by simply giving the area within myself that energy that I wanted to be a universe, intention and purpose—the purpose being to become what it wanted to be, what it felt was the best form it should undertake in all the frequencies and dimensions that it eventually settled on being. This resulted in the areas that eventually became physical in form moving away from each other to give themselves space, the space to not be influenced by each other in any significant way.

ME: *Are you suggesting that the galaxies and the universes have sentience, intelligence?*

SE: I am not suggesting it; they ARE sentient, they ARE intelligent, but they are not intellectual—they simply exist. In essence, the universes and the resulting galaxies are living entities in their own rights. Each universe that I created, twelve of them, have the power to manipulate themselves into the condition they feel best suits their own personal taste—the galaxies being the physical representation of what the universes have created within themselves.

ME: *I just got an image/suggestion that the galaxies are similar to cells within our human bodies.*

SE: That is not a bad description, for they are the more solid part of the universe's form, as it were, and they do have a function to perform within the structure of the universe. But to say that they were the cells of a larger form would be wrong, for the function that they have to perform is not the result of bodily function or the function of an organ within a larger body. Their function is to collect that energy that is close in frequency or dimension to the physical and give it form. In doing so, they clear all of the stray energies that are within their universe, the energies resulting from their initial manifestation or creation.

In essence, the objective of each of the galaxies is the grouping together of all of these energies into energy groups and giving them a purpose relative to the strengths and properties of their collective frequencies and energetic content. A good example of this can be seen in the physical bodies within what you call the solar system, the planets. Each of the planets is a grouping together of similar energies with each of the energies having a similar range of frequencies that manifest in a similar way in the lower dimensions—the similarity being enough to allow them to bind together. The result of such energies being similar but not quite the same is what you see in your periodic table. The earth is a classic example of this. It appears to be a solid lump in space made from the same material, but when you look deeper, you see that it is made up from a whole host of different materials that are only separated by frequency or a number of electrons. Sometimes only one frequency or electron will separate two different materials from each other when we synthesize them. Jupiter, on the other hand, is a classic example of a body that is a collection of higher frequency energies, the materials of which are gaseous in frequential representation in this dimension.

ME: *I have just gained a vision of a house made from bricks of different sizes, some being standard size , others being half size or double size—all of them being assembled together in a way that allows the house to be built and appear to be a single unit.*

SE: That is an excellent example and that is exactly what the galaxies are doing with the stray energies.

ME: *Is it fair to assume that at some point the galaxies were very small in comparison to what they are now?*

15

SE: Yes and no. Some of them started out at the large size they are now—their job being to collect the more subtle higher frequency energies. The smaller ones are more adept at gathering up the denser energies.

ME: *Like a black hole?*

SE: A black hole is, in fact, a small, very small galaxy. To do the job it has to do, it needs to be able to gather together energies that are right at the bottom of the frequencies of the dimensions they are working with. Hence, they have a lot of mass in comparison to their relative physical representation.

ME: *So this explains why the galaxies all have different shapes.*

SE: Yes, the shapes being relative to the energies they work with and the content of the energies they have managed to attract.

In fact, some of the energies they work with are so difficult to work with that they have to create constructs to aid collection specific to the energy type they are working with.

ME: *You mean like a machine?*

SE: No. This is an energetic construct; it is not physical at all. In fact, some of the constructs are so subtle they cannot be truly classified as a construct.

ME: *So what are they then if they are not whole enough to be classified as a construct?*

SE: They are more of an intention. Let me explain. Energies sometimes cannot be manipulated by physical or energetic means either alone or in total. This is because of the personality of the energy, for want of a better word. When the energy that is to be worked with does not respond to manipulation or transmutation, it means that the energy has personality. This means that the energy has a purpose of its own and will resist all changes that are intended to deviate it from this purpose. Thus, the energy needs to be persuaded to change the purpose of its existence to one that also includes the desire of the galactic entity. In doing this, it has to work with the energy for a long enough time for it to get used to the other energy that surrounds it or is close by to it. In essence, it needs to think of the galactic entity as part of it, even though it is not. The galactic entity, therefore, needs to manipulate its own base energy frequency and intention to one that is close enough to the signature energy of the energy to be attracted to allow it to be worked with whilst retaining enough of its own individuality to retain its own personality and beingness. Once the energy is "fooled" into thinking the galaxy is part of it, it is happy to have its intention changed to that of the galactic entity, provided that the galactic entity makes the changes to the intention in a subtle way that cannot be detected as an invasive energy.

ME: *So the galaxy, which is sort of an entity in its own right, has to fool the energy to be gathered that it is part of it and then re-program its intention/direction.*

SE: That's it. Although it is a really basic thing to talk about, in actuality, it can take many millennia to complete. This is why some galaxies appear to be big dust clouds with just a handful or, indeed, no material at all that is dense enough to call a star or, indeed, a planet. Hence some of the beautiful images that your Hubble space telescope has taken since its placement in earth orbit.

The Function of the Galaxies

ME: *So what other jobs do galaxies do other than collect stray energies?*

SE: They provide refuge for entities that have sought to be associated with the energies that have coalesced into the physical frequencies or those that might provide opportunity for higher entities' experience and evolution.

ME: *Hold on a bit. Are you suggesting that galactic entities, "galaxies," are fairly low down in the pecking order, entity-wise?*

SE: They are what they are. They are neither higher nor lower than other entities within my creativity. In essence, they are no different from you than I am from you. The only real difference is that they are of the group of entities that did not benefit as much as you and others like you did when I created you. In some respects, they are more important than you as they provide the opportunity for your growth and evolution, but in terms in their ability to experience, they are not nearly as nimble as you smaller, more agile entities.

ME: *So tell me more about what you meant by the galaxies providing refuge for the more agile entities.*

SE: The word "refuge" is a term of reference. It means place of security or place to live/exist. In essence, it is where the smaller, more compact and more agile/evolved entities can experience what they want to achieve to continue their evolutionary progression. This is where the galactic entities come into their own. Let me explain.

Their primary role is to gather stray energy and give it purpose. That purpose is to provide substance, substance for the evolution of the individualized entities. In doing this, they also progress evolution-wise—this progression being the result of their being of service to the individualized entities. In doing this, they help in progressing the bigger picture by helping the Origin to understand itself more and, in turn, evolve.

ME: *So the galactic entities are part of the plan as well?*

SE: Yes. Every entity I have created is both part of the plan and has a role to play within the plan. In performing their roles, they also progress and evolve.

18

Listen, the whole reason for all of our existence is to evolve—no question in that. Everyone, everything, every entity has a role to play in this, and we are enthusiastic in this role. In your exalted position of a free-thinking individualized entity, you are placed in a unique position to both assist in this goal and to accelerate it. But let me get back to the main answer to your question. The refuge given to you and the rest of the entities endowed with individuality is to provide the necessary theater for you to experience the things that you believe will result in your evolving in some (small) way. In your instance, this is by providing a physical location where you can experience a lower—much, much lower—level of existence than you would normally experience in your energetic state.

ME: *That's interesting because I don't seek greatness personally; I seek to be part of something great.*

SE: And this is exactly what you are doing in all of your work. This is the whole point of it—to recognize and be part of something great, and you are doing it so very well.

Let's get back to the refuge bit.

The refuge that the galaxy has created for all of the entities that are associated with this area of this particular dimension is peculiar to the opportunities for physical experience. Each of the physical entities that you call stars and planets give the opportunity for physical incarnation, that is, the opportunity to experience life or existence in a state lower in frequency that you would normally experience in your energetic state. This does not necessarily mean that you have to incarnate into the biological form you know as humankind, for it can be any mixture of materials that can be manipulated or given a level of autonomy whilst providing the ability to sustain and, therefore, be used as a host for an energetic entity.

ME: *So what part of a planet is the most useful in this sense?*

SE: From your perspective, the obvious mediums for physical and mobile existence are the air and water-based environments. However, there are also many opportunities to be gained in the rock, snow, molten rock, or metal-based environments. These are areas where you have not seriously considered that life, let alone sentient life, can exist.

ME: *You mean that entities can live in molten lava?*

SE: Yes, of course. Just because the medium for existence is not as human-friendly as you expect or require, it does not mean that it is barren of life. Life that is useful as a vehicle for incarnation into the physical comes in many guises.

ME: *What does the physical form that exists in lava look like?*

SE: First, physical form does not have to look like anything; second, it does not need to be in the lower frequencies that result in what you would call tangible form, for the physical also spans into the liquid and gaseous. It even goes so far as the level of radio wave frequencies. As you can imagine, the form that would exist in a lava flow would need to be able to traverse it without hindrance. An example would be the entities that exist in the heart of you sun. They are physical in nature but not in any way that you could imagine.

ME: *I have just picked up this image of intelligent life moving around in the maelstrom of the chemicals and metals of the super-heated soup that is at the center of the sun's core. They look like pure intelligence that moves from particle to particle. When they are all together, those particles give a slightly black hue compared to the yellow background glow of the sun's core, the only indication of the location and movement of the intelligence within this medium.*

SE: Very well done. This is a great observation and one that is highly accurate to boot. The intelligence as you call it is a race called the Grahoopnik, spoken in the human language as "Gra-Hoo-Pneekuh." Their prime point of existence is in the hearts of suns. They like the security and feeling of the energies within the core of suns, in particular, as they provide energies that are peculiar to the temperatures achieved in the gravitational forces that surround them.

ME: *Do they migrate or move from sun to sun?*

SE: Yes, of course. They do this instantaneously by logging into the signature of the energies they like best and moving on to the nearest sun that provides them.

ME: *I get the impression that they only move on when they have removed all of the energies they like from the sun they are currently in.*

SE: Yes, that is true.

ME: *Can I ask a leading question? Do these entities cause suns to explode and turn into super novas?*

SE: That is sometimes the result of their existence and vacating their last point of reference, yes.

ME: *Will our sun go super nova as a result of their residence and ultimate leaving?*

SE: Yes, it will, but do not worry. Humankind in its current form will be long gone a millennia before as it will have progressed beyond the need for the particular type of physicality that it currently uses for its evolutionary vehicle. The physical demise of both the sun and the solar system will occur; your current Earth will no longer exist as you know it to be.

ME: *Do you mean it will disappear totally, or will it change to some other energetic form?*

SE: The Earth and the rest of the planets in the solar system will have translated to their next level of evolution before the sun's physical presence is removed. In fact, the energies released from the sun as a result of the existence of the Grahoopnik within the sun will be the catalyst for frequential progression. In their living and migrating from

21

sun to sun, they can leave a trail of what you in the physical call "destruction," but they can also leave what we in the energetic call "areas of progression." Therefore, the Earth will only die in physical terms; it will not die in energetic terms. This is also your future heritage.

ME: *In effect, you are saying that the Grahoopnik have an important and symbiotic relationship with the human race's opportunity for evolutionary progression?*

SE: They inadvertently assist in the frequential progression of many physical races, and they will assist in the progression of humankind as well. But please take note on what I said before. Humankind will be long gone from the physical when the sun physically dies since the energies that are released that assist in the increase in frequency happen a long time before physical dissolution/demise. In fact, some of you will note that a change in frequency is already happening. This is both a result of humankind's natural progression and the local existence of the Grahoopnik in your sun.

ME: *Yes, a number of well-known mediums have been saying this for some years, but they only attribute it to the increase in humans who are becoming aware and not as an additional result of an outside force, such as the Grahoopnik.*

SE: No, they would not know that. They could not know that, for they are not expansive enough in their mediumship.

ME: *Why not?*

SE: Because they only look for what is in the human mind and not what is in the universal mind, so they miss the rest of the detail. This is a great shame, for there is much, much more that needs to be transmitted to mankind. I can only do this through people like you.

ME: *Thank you.*

Galaxies—A Force for Change

ME: O.K., so we have talked about the galaxies as being a refuge for the development of many physical races—some of which, like the Grahoopnik, exist within extreme environments on the edge of physicality that humankind does not even recognize as such. We have even talked about the other roles of galaxies, such as the gathering up of stray energies. What else do they have to do in the bigger picture?

SE: They are the guardians of the space that they exist within; this is their main role. They are given complete autonomy in this and answer to no one but myself. If you consider that the universes I created are the playground of the more intelligent entities, so to speak, a playground of evolutionary opportunity, then you will realize that this playground needs to be nurtured, looked after, and modified to best suit the needs of the entities that are using it. This is the role of the galaxies: to look at the physical opportunities that they present to the entities that are in existence for purely evolutionary existence, such as yourself, and modify themselves upon demand to offer the best experiences possible. By "on demand," I mean that the galaxy has the ability to look inwardly and see where the areas for improvement are and amend itself accordingly.

ME: Do you mean that the galaxies are able to change their look and feel locally or globally on a daily basis, or do they only change when the opportunity is best offered to them by the activities of the entities within them?

SE: They generally wait for a significant event to happen that will give the opportunity for change more impetuous. If the change was to be on a daily basis, you would witness the disappearance/appearance of stars and planets or, in fact, the location or re-location of new or existing stars and planets. Let me make one thing clear though.

Changes generally happen over a long period of time as the affected races need the time to adapt and adjust to their new environment. It is rare that a change is required on an instantaneous timeframe. This is not to say that it can't be done. It has, but a change of such a level requires a complete evacuation of all the existing entities within the area to be changed, which, of course, requires some planning since many of the entities are incarnate in the physical to a level similar to yourself. Thus, the evacuation has to be staged in a way that is consistent with their normal return to the energetic.

ME: So how would you engage in an instantaneous evacuation of incarnate entities to make a change?

SE: By catastrophe.

ME: What?

SE: By catastrophe. By far the fastest way to evacuate a large number of incarnate entities is to evoke a catastrophe. This would allow the change to be made directly after the last entity to leave the physical is properly back in the energetic.

ME: But isn't a catastrophe a rather harsh way of making a change?

SE: Not in the slightest. It is not used for fun, but when it is deemed necessary, it is used without issue by any of the entities involved. For many of them, the mere act of being part of such an event comes high on their evolutionary experience list. You on Earth have already experienced two such events on a very local level—one of them you even have racial memory of; you call it the "great flood."

ME: Are you saying that the great flood was the result of our galaxy affecting a change on the earth to make it a better place to evolve in?

SE: That's about the size of it, yes. You see, at that point in time, the earth required a change in biosphere type to enable the ratio of water and land-based entities to be adjusted in accordance with the number of incarnate entities it could support. In the earth's instance, there needed to be an increase in the area of water to allow the water-based entities to increase in number. This required a dramatic reduction in the land that was available and a suitable reduction in the maximum number of land-based entities.

ME: The change was to allow more dolphins to be incarnate?

SE: The dolphin physicality is but one of the many water-based entities that offer the opportunity for incarnation into the physical. There are many more water-based entities in your seas than you are aware of. A great many of them live in the semi-physical states and are, therefore, not readily detectable. Some keep themselves very much to themselves whilst others live in parts of the ocean that is so deep you simply have not been down there long enough to see them.

ME: So how many land-based entities were evacuated, so to speak?

SE: Approximately 20 billion.

ME: 20 billion. We don't have that many people on the earth now, and we are quite advanced.

SE: Don't forget that the ratio of land mass to water mass was significantly different at that time. In fact, the water mass was 20-30% of what it is now, so there was a lot of land for the land-based entities to live on.

ME: And they all just rolled over and accepted the change?

SE: Yes. They knew at the energetic (higher self) level that the change was necessary, and, as such, their souls were ready to leave. When the time came, they dissolved their links with their physical vehicles and returned to the energetic en mass. The physical vehicles were not left behind, of course, as they were returned to their core elements during dissolution. Only a few of the incarnate land-based entities elected to stay. In doing so, they had to create a number of vehicles to protect their physical bodies, including a core volume of the species most necessary to protect the continuation of the flora and fauna. What you would call an ARK.

ME: *And all of the incarnate entities knew that they needed to dissolve themselves to allow this change for the better?*

SE: Yes, and what's more some of them were architects in the need to make the change. These were also the ones that stayed behind to commence the re-building.

ME: *This is a good example of a small local change. What about a large change?*

SE: A large change is far too big for you to understand as it takes a significant amount of time to plan and involves whole sectors of space, not just a particular planet or planetary system. Because of this I will give you an example of a medium sized change that a galaxy may wish to undertake.

ME: *How big would this be?*

SE: Several planets, and, in some instances, more than one planetary system. It would certainly include the local star, which would be involved from its own evolutionary perspective due to the very nature of the physical reaction necessary to make the change.

ME: *What are you suggesting? Oh, I get it. The star is going nova.*

SE: Well done. The nova state is, in fact, the smaller of the two events that could be described as a medium-sized change and the slightly larger being what you describe as a supernova.

ME: *So what is the difference between the two, apart from the obvious fact that one is bigger than the other?*

SE: The nova-sized influence involves only one star. The second, the supernova, is much bigger and can involve a number of stars.

I will explain this further.

A nova is used to make a change in the area local to the star being used as the catalyst. It generally only involves the planetary entities and those entities that are associated with those planets close to the star. You see a nova as a destructive force with the star exploding and destroying the planets close to it and any life on those planets. The sun later is reduced to a white dwarf when all the energy is spent, the area then being dead. This is not the case since what is happening is both of a housekeeping nature to the galaxy and an evolutionary nature to the physical bodies involved. You see, if the galaxy needs to make a change that involves the star and its wards, its planets— remember that both are energetic entities on their own right—the galaxy offers the star two options. These options greatly depend on the evolutionary condition of the star and its planets, which will include the work that the smaller entities, such as you (humankind), has achieved to date. If the star and its planets/inhabitants are ready for an evolutionary change that is beneficial to them, then the star will undergo a change that increases the local frequency enough for them all to move on to the next level. The process is what your astronomers observe as a nova. In essence, the star, with the aid of the galaxy, increases its frequency to the point where it appears to explode, destroying the planets that are associated with it, leaving only debris, spent fuel, the dwarf star, and asteroids. In reality what has happened is that they have all moved up to the next frequency level, leaving behind the untranslatable physical aspects of themselves. In essence, they have given up their physicality, all of them, all together.

ME: *Would not the inhabitants of the planets/star move upwards through the frequencies first with the star and the planets following them?*

SE: No, this is not part of the process. Simplistically put, they all move onwards and upwards together. To not do so would be like moving from a house without a house to go to for the first couple of days of the move. It would not be synchronous. This is important as it maintains the balance between that which has progressed in the frequencies, that which remains, and that which is governed for in the spatial/dimensional planning.

In the event that the star and its planets/inhabitants are not yet ready to move upwards in the frequencies, they are moved to a new location in keeping with the plan the galaxy has for its own evolution and housekeeping.

ME: *You mean to say that whole solar systems are moved to somewhere else?*

SE: Yes, this is quite common.

ME: *How long does this take?*

SE: It is instantaneous. However, it is the product of a significant amount of planning on behalf of the galaxy and the star and must also be of benefit to them as well. Both methods require planning, and all inhabiting entities are involved from an awareness point of view. They are also given help from the entities in the locale where they are moving because the inclusion of a new star system has an effect on them as well. Consider the gravitational effects from both the attractivity of physical mass and the changes to the communication aspect that the change to the gravity profile in the receiving area has. It all has to be planned.

ME: *We could talk about this for a very long time.*

SE: The detail of this could only briefly be described, for it would require many volumes to do it justice.

ME: *So what about supernovas?*

SE: Supernovas are basically a bigger version of what I have just described. The only issue here is that we are not just talking about the opportunity to move multiple star systems. Change of this magnitude means that the opportunity for physical relocation is not only unnecessary but is not even considered. In essence, the supernova method of increasing the frequencies of the star/planetary and inhabiting entities in this area is a result of the whole area being ready to move upwards. This is usually the product of a significant length of time where all of the entities in the area, star/planetary and incumbent dimensional beings, have been working together to increase their evolutionary condition to the point where the galaxy has taken the opportunity to make both the opportunity and plans to lift that part of itself up to the next level.

ME: *I have just received the image of a galaxy moving parts of itself up to the next level of frequency on a gradual basis, one bit at a time, rather like putting a frame tent up.*

SE: This is a good analogy and is what happens in most examples. However, there are a small number of galaxies who move everything associated with them up to the next frequency level simultaneously, but this needs every entity associated with that galaxy to be on the same evolutionary flight path, so to speak.

This is difficult to maintain and control—not from a "translation up the frequencies" point of view but from a "control of the equilibrium" of the areas that are *ready* to be translated versus those that are *close to* being translated but could drop backwards in the frequencies and, therefore, put the translation at risk.

Planets, the Workforce of the Galaxies

ME: *We have reviewed the way you created the universe/s and the work that the galaxies perform. We have even discussed the role that some of the entities that live in the stars have and what the stars do to help the galaxies change local areas of space to a condition that is better suited to the evolution of the evolutionary process in the physical planes and the closest energetic planes. I would now like to discuss the roles the planets have in this work.*

SE: First, let me remind you that as with all physical bodies in the physical universe that are but a small portion of what they represent in the energetic, so the work the galaxies and the stars perform in the physical is also manifested in the energetic. This is the same for the planets, for they are also entities in their own right.

ME: *So let me get the chronology right before we start on the planets' roles.*

You created the universes to provide an environment for a smaller set of entities to exist within. This level of creation formed energies that manifest itself in all levels of frequency in all dimensions within each of the universes in various forms, some of which are within the frequencies we humans call the physical. These energies, including those in the physical were given form and awareness of self, beginning and recognition of source, you the Source Entity. Responsible to you, they were then given roles and responsibilities to ensure the maintenance of their environment would be kept to an optimal. Part of this involved the opportunity for their own evolution since they were given individuality, though coadunate with you. In the maintenance of their environment, they tidy up the manifested physical form energies into energies similar to their own frequencies—thus, creating galaxies. As galaxies they further their work by concentrating on the smaller energies and collate them into stars and planets— some stars and planets being attracted to each other, others not. When the planets are of a certain size or energetic density that is enough to endow them with retention of memory and recognition of self, they gain awareness, self-awareness, and recognition structure of

30

others like them. They are then give roles and responsibilities in keeping with those of their galaxy.

SE: Very good summary. As soon as they achieved this last part, I released the remaining entities such as yourself into the universes I created. All of you have three main things embedded within your consciousness:

1. Recognition of self (awareness);
2. Recognition of origin (me, your Source Entity) and position within a hierarchy;
3. Recognition of goal (to experience and evolve as a result).

Some of you have a fourth item embedded within your consciousness—freewill.

ME: I thought we were all created at the same time?

SE: You were, but I held my most precious creations back until I was satisfied the environment had achieved a minimal level of structure before introducing you to it. Now let's get back to the planets.

The role of the planets is threefold: 1) to provide a smaller cleaning/gathering function by attracting denser energies and integrating them; 2) to provide a focal point for the physical and energetic existence of smaller energetic entities; 3) to experience and evolve in their own right. In doing these three things, they provide the most basic functions for the continued function of the universe for they are the workers at the "coal face," so to speak. They are the origin and the creator of what you call nature spirits. In fact, they are nature spirits in their own right.

ME: What do you mean? Are you saying that the planet performs a similar role in the solar system/galaxy that the nature spirits on Earth itself perform—like maintenance of the lower life forms, such as trees and rocks?

31

SE: Absolutely. Know this: every entity in the universe/s I have created has a role to play in the maintenance of their locale—whether it be collecting stray energy, keeping the frequencies of the energy as high as possible, providing a refuge for physical existence for the smaller energy beings, or simply evolving themselves. As an example of some of Earth's physical work in the space it occupies, you only need see the aurora borealis, the "northern lights." These are a physical manifestation of the cleaning-up exercise that Earth performs in removing and converting local levels of cosmic energy that are detrimental to the functionality of physical beings on Earth's plane and disturb the clarity of communication between the entity you call the sun and those entities whose job it is to maintain the direction of "solar wind." Solar wind is used by "star" entities to exchange energies—other than those that are self-generated—with other star entities. In essence, the planets have one of the most important jobs in the universe. They have a responsibility to those smaller entities that use their surfaces for the existence of their physical vehicles by making sure they maintain the ecosystem at the most optimal possible condition—even when they are making changes to themselves to enable energetic adaptations to take place.

A planet's contribution to the evolution game is at its most effective when it houses more than two sentient/high level energy being types in the energetic, the physical, or both simultaneously. In fact, the more entity types it can support, the more effective its contribution, and the faster it can evolve in its own right.

ME: *So how many entities does Earth currently support?*

SE: Three, plus the visitors of which there are over twenty different types.

ME: Let me guess the three: humans, dolphins, and another animal of some sort?

SE: We have discussed this in some shape or form before, especially about the fact that dolphins are one of the other races that are using Earth for evolutionary purposes. The third is purely energetic and exists in an area in one of your seas that is secluded from mankind but not from the dolphins. In fact, the dolphins communicate with this third race on a very regular basis.

ME: Does mankind communicate with them on some secret basis?

SE: Energetically, you know of their existence, of course, but from the view point of physical mankind you have no idea of their existence and have never seen or felt their presence.

ME: Will we ever meet them?

SE: Only when mankind as a collective affects a change in their frequency level to the point where physical incarnation is no longer necessary.

ME: Will this be soon?

SE: It will not be in several hundred physical lifetimes. Before this can happen, the frequency of Earth has to be raised seven frequency levels, and this can only be done when the human race decides to give up the need for personal gratification and is more concerned about his fellow man and always puts his neighbor first. At this point mankind will work on an individual level/basis for the good of the whole without the need for catastrophes to act as a catalyst for communal working. Even now catastrophes don't work that well because so-called celebrities use them for their own ends by purporting to be concerned about the safety and well-being of those affected when really all they are doing is using the catastrophes as an opportunity for publicity. Do not *seek* to be a celebrity! It is a sure fire way to slow your evolution down.

33

But let's get back to the role of planets. As stated recently, a planet as an entity in its own right contributes significantly to the maintenance of its locale. Part of that maintenance occurs as a result of its own evolution. As a planet literally gives itself up for the benefit of others, its opportunity for evolutionary advancement is massive and so is the opportunity to affect an increase in frequency in the locale. However, it is also affected by the frequency changes made by those entities it hosts, and in Earth's instance, it simply has not caught up with the loss of frequency caused by mankind's mistakes.

ME: *So a planet's role is to provide habitation, clean up energies that are harmful to those inhabitants, and maintain certain communication lines between the star entities and those that work with the solar winds.*

SE: That is a short and sweet way of putting it, yes. But they have one more role.

ME: *What is that?*

SE: To add substance to the fabric of the universe in both the energetic and physical frequency levels. Essentially they are the glue that holds it all together.

The Creation and Roles of Smaller Entities

ME: *As you said in the first book, you created billions of smaller entities to experience and evolve as part of the creation process of the universe/s. The objective was/is to experience existence at the largest/smallest possible level and at the highest/lowest possible frequency.*

I have to admit that I was very surprised to learn that we were kept on the back burner, so to speak, until you had stabilized—if that is the right word—the universe.

SE: Stabilization is a necessary part of the process of creation.

Had I introduced you all at a point just after the creation of the universe/s, you would have been swept away in the maelstrom that resulted from the coalescence of the energies. You would have lost your datum dimension and frequency level as well as your direction, especially since the galaxies were working on shepherding energies on all dimensions on all frequencies simultaneously. It was a tumultuous period and one that needed its own time to complete. So the smaller entities, such as you, had to wait in a holding area until the environment was ready for you to move into.

ME: *So what did we do whilst in this holding area?*

SE: Nothing.

ME: *Nothing?*

SE: Nothing. You see, although I had created you all, none of you were in a position to recognize your "self." You had no self-awareness and, therefore, achieved nothing. In actual fact, if one or two of you had started to develop awareness, I would have held you in stasis because relocation to your new dimension so quickly after becoming aware of your initial surroundings would have been somewhat confusing to you.

ME: *Why would it have been confusing? I thought that we are just smaller versions of your self and that we are able to work with most, if not all, the energies in your universe?*

SE: This is very true, but the issue was that the area of holding was a very limited dimensional/frequential resource and, therefore, of little stimulation. The length of time you were in the holding area was such that if you were aware, you would have tuned into the limitations of that area of habitation and adapted to it. To have done so at such an early part of your existence would have meant that you would have programmed yourselves to be smaller than your potential. You would have been like the fish that grows to suit the size of the pond, so to speak; you would be stunted with very little chance of recovery.

35

ME: *Why would we not have recovered?*

SE: When I created you all, I gave you the ability to expand to the limits of your abilities in the universe that I was creating, a sort of automatic one time program designed to make you automatically become the best you will ever be functionally but with the ability to grow as individuals, to evolve. If this program/process started, you would have expanded to the abilities that you would have been capable of achieving in the holding area, which was extremely limiting. Fortunately, none of you had been created for very long, just a few millennia, and, therefore, had not achieved self-awareness and therefore kicked off the program of expansion.

ME: *Tell me more about this program. What else did it contain?*

SE: Apart from attunement to the dimensions and the frequencies that are associated with the universes that I created—which in itself gives you your expansiveness—it also identified the level of entity you were—remember we discussed the fact that some of the entities I created were not of the same type due my attention not being equally spread amongst my creations during the creativity process—and where you would be best located dimensionally. Those that were "whole" were allowed to expand to the level where they could work in any of the environments, dimensions/frequencies within the universal expanse whilst others were limited to smaller areas. Once they were attuned, the next part started: the realization of self, which also started the recognition of others and the interaction with others. The objective here was that the entities would achieve more if the recognition of self and others was simultaneous. Coupled together with this was the knowledge of the need to experience as much as possible and to evolve as a consequence. Next, the knowledge of position within the universe was made accessible, including their mission in existence and the understanding of who the Origin is and why it created the twelve Source Entities. Finally, knowing that individuality is maintained even in oneness and the desire to return to Source, bringing back all experiences, was ingrained into the memory.

ME: *The parts of the programming that you have just mentioned are these:*

- *Realization of self;*
- *Recognition of others;*
- *Experiencing existence;*
- *Evolving;*
- *Recognizing one's position within the universe;*
- *Recognizing one's mission in existence;*
- *Understanding the Origin and its creations;*
- *Returning to the Source when appropriate;*
- *Maintaining oneness whilst in the whole/source.*

These are essentially what our role is in the universe. This is all we have to do. It's simple.

SE: Not as simple as it would seem. Remember we talked about karma in the previous dialogues in your first book. Remember about being coerced by the desires of the physical and how easy it was to get tied up in the demands of the physical to the point where you no longer work for the good of others but only for yourself?

ME: *Yes, I do.*

SE: Well, this is a reason why it is not so simple. It's also one of the main reason why you, the smaller entities, were created. On behalf of myself and the Origin, you were all created to tackle the issue of "self," which all of the former bulleted items identify. In summary, the main role of all of the smaller entities in existence is to experience that which the Origin hasn't yet experienced and relay this information back to the Origin. In essence, the Origin has hatched a brilliant plan: as you experience, so do I and so does the Origin. What's more with all of the billions of entities the other twelve Source Entities and I have created, the opportunity for experiencing its self—for we are all within and, therefore, part of the Origin—is multiplied by a factor relative to the number of smaller entities created and actively experiencing. The one thing you must note is that there is no duplication here. Every experience is separate.

ME: *Why is this? I would have thought that, if say, 100 entities all experienced the same thing, such as a natural disaster or a football match, that it would amount to the same thing.*

SE: This is not so. It is the underlying beauty of being a separate entity. You see, even if you are part of a collective and you experience the same thing as your brother in collective existence, you each will personally experience the experience in a subtly different way. The way in which you experience it will be relevant to your own evolution and experience in addition to whether you are incarnate or not or the type of environment you have been incarnate in. Remember: incarnation isn't necessarily in a state that is as physically dense or in as low a frequency as you are experiencing now, for physicality has many levels of frequency. In summary, the whole point of existence and, therefore, the role of the smaller entities are to experience, evolve, furnish feedback, and return.

Chapter 2

Source Entity Two

At this point I have to admit to feeling a significant amount of trepidation. I am about to communicate with another of the Source Entities, one that we shall call Source Entity Two (SE2). The Creator of our multiverse being Source Entity One but simplistically being referred to as "The Source Entity" (SE). It is a strange feeling, rather like having writer's block. I have no idea what we are going to talk about even though I do have a simple agenda of questions, which I shall use for discussions with all the Source Entities. This should keep it simple, as I am in no doubt that many of the concepts that I am about to have thrust upon me will be well over my head. I only hope I can put them into words that both the readers of this text and I can understand.

ME: *I feel the communication start, but it feels strange—like I am rubbing my head up and down the bark of an oak tree.*

SE: That is because you are trying to communicate with the Source, SE2, directly rather than via myself. You are created from my own energies; these are in variance to the energies that the other Source Entities are working with. As a result, it will be like hitting a brick wall, for you are out of tune, out of phase, and out of (universal) structure. I am not surprised you feel like you are rubbing your head up and down the bark of an oak tree. What I am surprised about is that you even got to this stage; you actually made a link directly to SE2. I am impressed; this will make our communication with SE2 much easier as the level of translatory intervention I will have to make will be reduced as a result. Don't get me wrong. I will still need to be the main contact, and in most cases you will be communicating with SE2 via me, but in the link you have you will be able to pick up much more than SE2 speaking through my words to you. You may also gain imagery during the dialogue.

ME: *So can you tell me how this Source Entity divided itself?*

SE: Yes. In this instance, SE2 divided itself in a very similar way to the way I did, but it divided itself up by four instead of twelve, so, in effect, you have 12x4x12x3 different dimensional levels. That is 1,728 dimensions within four universes.

ME: *So would this similarity be the reason why I was able to affect some sort of initial communication?*

SE: No. Just because the methodology of division is similar doesn't mean that the frequencies and dimensions within the environment created have the same characteristics— hence, the way you felt when you established contact on your own.

ME: *Thank you for the clarification. So can you formally introduce me to the second source, SE2?*

SE: Yes. We are in contact right now.

ME: *Oh, I feel that I am in an environment that is full of green/grey/red clouds.*

SE2: These are my children. You would call them nebula. They form the larger part of the beings that I have created.

ME: *O.K. I think I would like to stop here and ask that I follow a structure that is similar, if not the same, to the first part of this book. It would keep it simple for me and those who read it later.*

SE2: We can do that if you wish.

ME: *I am sorry to mention it, but you sound like you are in pain. Your voice sounds like it is deep and hollow.*

SE2: I can assure you that I am not in pain. The sound of my voice, the method that you have chosen to communicate by, is relative to my overall resonant frequency. This is the way that you will be able to tell me apart from your own Source Entity.

Source Entity Two's Early Existence

ME: *I have talked to my Source Entity on its becoming aware in the first period of its existence. Can you explain how you became aware and what you felt?*

SE2: As with your own Source Entity, I was allowed to become aware in my own time. This is one of the rules the Origin placed upon itself. It was a strange sensation. Becoming aware that you "are" in existence is rather like looking at a cloud of energy and then realizing that it is a cloud of energy. As you start to pick out things in your local environment and identify them by giving them a name or a label, you start to consider who and what you are yourself. At this point I started to investigate my "self" and realized that it was a big task, especially if I looked into my "self" at the smallest level. It was during this phase of my existence—when I was becoming more aware of what I was and what I could do—that the Origin contacted me and explained that I was a smaller part of its "self." It was also at this time I had established that there were others like me just next door.

ME: *Yes, I get an image of you all bunched up together, like black balls all together inside a bigger ball—that bigger ball being the Origin.*

41

Figure 1: The Origin and the Source Entities

SE2: That is a good description. But don't forget that the Origin is absolute and infinite, there is nothing but the Origin, the Origin is "all," so this image in your mind's eye that shows the Origin as a smaller entity is flawed and is a result of your limited ability to understand in your current projection.

ME: So what did the Origin say to you when it contacted you for the first time?

SE2: It explained the reason for my existence and the reason for the other Source Entities' existence. This you have from your own Source Entity. More importantly it stated that how I achieve the task it gave me was entirely up to me. There were no time limits and no constraints on power or energy used. It was a simple meeting. The Origin went to some length to make it so and to show me what the Origin was in its entirety just so that I could understand what it was and what I was and how I fitted in. Once the Origin had explained everything that it knew to me, I felt that I was one and the same. I was the

Origin, which as a division of the Origin we all are. As a result of this, I had what you might call a "kick-start" in the right direction. The change in me was instantaneous. One moment I was just me in existence and thought; the next moment, that is after the Origin gave me all its knowledge, I was personified. I was energy and thought, given knowledge and a purpose: to find out what I was, to experience what I was, and to evolve. As I was a part of the Origin, everything I did would be automatically fed back to the Origin in an experiential way, so I wouldn't need to contact the Origin specifically to report back on the progress I was making. It was at this point that I started to have what you would call "fun" by manipulating the energy that was all around us. I was particularity good at making shapes and dimensional constructs.

ME: *So how did you decided on the 12x4x12x3 dimensional universe?*

SE2: I decided that I would create four environments from which to base my learning environment on simply because I wanted to have four different experiments running at the same time. Each universe—if you want to call the environments that—were constructed in a different way. Each had a different purpose and a different set of rules.

ME: *You had a different set of rules for each environment? Why? What were the rules?*

SE2: I wanted to see how the entities that I would create later in order to populate these environments would fare if they had a different set of constraints placed on them, but with the same goal. One of the environments—let's call it environment one for the sake of argument—had no constraints and had all the abilities I had. The others had components of those abilities removed.

The Four Environments of SE2

Environment 1—10,000 Source Entities, One Environment

ME: *Can you explain what the abilities and components were that you removed? No, tell me about the first environment first, and then tell me what the constraints were in the remaining three environments.*

SE2: As just stated, the first environment contained every attribute that I was given by the Origin. Everything was within the environment right down to the lowest dimension and frequency. Additionally, the entities that I created were direct copies of me, only smaller in what you would call volume. They were constrained, however, in one way: they could only exist within the environment that I created. That is, they could not return to the Source, me, as you can with your own Source Entity.

ME: *Why did you do that? What would be the point of it?*

SE2: I wanted to give them total autonomy. With the level of power that I had given them, equal to me, they could quite literally turn their environment upside down and inside out. I wanted them to know this and to appreciate that they would have no help from me in correcting whatever mess they got themselves into and that they were the masters of their own destiny, whichever way they took themselves.

ME: *So what was the goal that you gave them?*

SE2: The goal or task was the same as yours. We all have the same task from the Origin: to experience all that there is in as many different ways as possible and evolve as a result.

ME: *But you have given them everything and nothing. You have given them a task and not a route home—to you.*

SE2: I have given them everything. They have total autonomy from me, they are masters of their own universe, and they will exist for as long as I exist.

ME: *And how long will you exist?*

SE2: For as long as the Origin wants us to exist. It has no plans to remove that existence to my knowledge, but my/our/your existence is still at the prerogative of the Origin and its pleasure in my/our/your existence.

ME: *Mmm, O.K., I think I have been advised on this subject before by my Source Entity.*

SE: You have, and it is a consistent story that you will hear from all of the Source Entities.

ME: *It is good to realize that you are still here and that I can recognize you as my Source Entity.*

SE: Yes, don't forget that I still need to support the link you have with SE2, which is why you are finding it so easy to communicate with it.

ME: *Thank you. So, getting back to the first environment from SE2's experiments, can you please give me an example of the type of power these entities had in the first environment?*

SE2: As explained a few moments ago, they had total power. But I can see that you need an example. Quite simply, they have the power to either totally destroy themselves by refusing to exist anymore or they can reproduce themselves or their environment.

ME: *Reproduction of self I can understand, but reproduction of environment, whole universe/multiverses? Why would they want to do that? How would they do it?*

SE2: How they do it is up to them, but one way would be to segment a portion of the environmental volume that I gave them to create a duplicate. Another way would be to mirror the whole volume of the environment by copying it and placing it on a level of dimension or frequency that is just out of alignment with the original.

ME: *But would you need to remove a frequential or dimensional component from the existing environment to achieve this?*

SE2: Good question. No, you are thinking in terms of your own environment and its physical physics. The way it would be achieved is by . . .

ME: *I am getting a picture of a sort of process where you make better use of the space available; err, rather like a double space program on a computer makes more space on a hard drive by using a form of compression algorithm that maintains all of the attributes of the files on the hard drive whilst making them smaller, thereby saving space.*

SE2: That wasn't the description I was going to use, but it is one that will suffice. It is a good enough example for your readers to understand. In fact, it is possibly the only way that you will be able to understand the process.

ME: *Why is this?*

SE2: I was having trouble embedding the information into your limited energetic memory. It just wasn't capable of receiving the concept I was prepared to give to you. Multiversal compression is a good enough example to use.

ME: *So if the entities within Environment 1 are all powerful, they must have a hard time living together.*

SE2: They do not fight if that is what you are insinuating. They each have the same capabilities and they have full respect of their role within their environment.

ME: *How many entities did you create for the first environment?*

SE2: You would call it a round number and, therefore, suspicious.

ME: *Go on. Try me.*

SE2: Ten thousand.

ME: *You're right. It is a round number and I am suspicious.*

SE2: ?

ME: *What? Is that it? Silence?*

SE2: What would you have me say? Do you want me to give you justification for such a whole number?

ME: *Err, yes actually. I had a similar issue with the number of levels that my Source Entity created. They were based on 100.*

SE2: One of the things that you must note is that the numbers that I/we use are in the language that you would understand. I/we use whole numbers because of the ease of communication. Suffice to say, the number I gave you is correct and as such is understandable by you and others. Would a number of 9,892 have any more credence with you?

ME: *It might.*

SE2: Then use that. It is not correct, for it was 10,000.

ME: *O.K., I think I will leave this little digression in the text of this dialogue; the mere fact that you are questioning my questioning is validation enough for me.*

SE: Rest now. You are tired.

A few days later I continued the conversation.

ME: *Can we continue with the first of the four environments you created?*

SE2: Yes, of course.

ME: *One of the questions that I have not asked is about the appearance of the entities in this environment and what they created as a civilization.*

SE2: I will answer your question in two parts. In terms of their appearance, they have none that you would recognize.

ME: *How do you mean?*

SE2: They do not have a physical appearance. I can see that you are waiting for further clarification.

ME: *Yes, please.*

SE2: They have no method of being described physically because the environment within which they exist does not have dimensions or frequencies that are low enough to cause a physical projection. Simply put: they are purely "Source Essence" and so is their environment.

ME: *Hold on here. I have just received an image or concept in my mind that states that they are all one and the same—that is, their environment and the entities are all one.*

SE2: That is correct. That is why they have no form, either physical or energetic, that you can use to distinguish them apart from their environment.

ME: *Is this why you only created 10,000?*

SE2: Yes, it is also why I gave them total autonomy. They are as I am within my own environment, totally omnipotent.

ME: *So how do you tell them apart? Do they have a signature or something that enables you to identify which one of the ten thousand they are?*

SE2: They can only be told apart by their thought processes. Each one has a different thought process that they use to create the opportunity to experience and evolve. But please note this: not all of them are in full separate existence at the same time.

ME: *I beg your pardon? You mean that one moment they are in existence and another they are not?*

SE2: As you noted before, they are one and the same and, therefore, one with their environment. I see you are frowning. I will send you an image of what I mean.

I then received an image of a mass of something, say a cloud. This cloud was on its own as an undulating mass. Then I saw a mass of what I can only describe as rain drops. Each rain drop had its own sentience. As I looked further and into the cloud, which I was told was their environment, I noticed that each of the drops had a role to play and a job to do. Each role and job was either personally assigned or collectively assigned. Before the role/job was assigned, the rain drop that was to do the role was not a separate entity. It was fully part of the cloud. When the role was defined and the interaction with other raindrops or energies was established, a rain drop or a series of rain drops would be formed, and they would do what was necessary to perform and complete the task. When the task was complete, the rain drop or drops would return to the cloud and lose their singularity. They became one with the cloud again. Their singularity was lost, but their essence was maintained within the cloud, the/their environment. The cloud, the environment, was built of Source Essence that could be separated into two parts: environmental essence and individualized essence.

Figure 2: The Cloud and Rain Drops

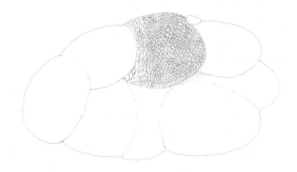

SE2: Now do you understand how they exist?

ME: Yes, I think I do. That image was a really simple and effective way of describing what they are. I take it that there are no clouds or rain drops—that was just a method to describe the function of environment and individualized energy, a way to explain in simple terms how there can be a "variance" in the number of entities in existence, for want of a better word. It's a way to show that there never are all of the entities you created within this environment in singular existence at any one time, or are there times?

SE2: There have been times, and there will be times when they are all in existence as single entities all together, so to speak. Such a time is when they are all needed to change the characteristics of the environment within which they exist, for this can only be achieved when all are in agreement.

ME: Yes, I appreciate that would be a limitation. So what about civilization? Do they have one? Did they create one?

SE2: Civilization is a word that is peculiar to your physical-based existence. It determines that entities or beings behave in a way that you classify as civilized, that a certain level of co-operation and technology is present and the level of technology is a product of the level of co-operation on a personal and group basis. I am correct in this assumption?

ME: Yes, you are.

SE2: Well, in this instance you can say that the entities and the environment within which they exist are civilized.

ME: What? Is that it? Was there no creativity or area/environment which a group of them created for the betterment of them all and that has stood the test of time to show that they were, in fact, civilized and could be called a civilization, and that it was successful or failed?

SE2: Not in the way that you perceive things, no. For how could a group of entities that are essentially Source Essence and part of an environment that is created out of Source Essence become something that they have always been—in co-operation?

ME: *You mean they have never become uncivilized/ they have never failed to achieve their goal, a goal that if it failed would have resulted in some form of digression between the entities involved.*

SE2: No. You see, even when they have failed to achieve the goal that they set themselves, they have managed to learn something, they have experienced something, they have evolved in some way.

ME: *I suppose in this instance if the entities concerned really are one and the same with themselves and their environment and are also truly omnipotent, they would behave in a civilized way.*

SE2: The correct description would be that they behave in a highly evolved way, for each of them is aware of the power they have singularly, collectively, and environmentally. They are aware of their function within the environment and the group and have nothing to gain or lose by "going it alone." However, they have had a number of experiments where only one or two of them would split off from the whole and work alone.

ME: *What was the outcome of these experiments?*

SE2: That they are more efficient at evolving by doing things as a whole. They did find evolution singularly an interesting concept, but it was detrimental to the evolution of the whole.

Environment 2—The Cast-out Principle

ME: *O.K., let's move on to the second environment that you created. What limitations did you put on the environment and its inhabitants?*

SE2: In this instance I allowed them the opportunity to return to their source if they wished. They could/can also return to singularity if they wish/wished. In this they are similar to you but only in this instance.

ME: *How do you mean?*

SE2: They don't have free will like you do.

ME: *What other limitations do they have?*

SE2: They are not omnipotent in their own environment like the entities in the first environment. They can create, and they can destroy, but they cannot manipulate their own environment in any way. Also they are limited to one dimension and one frequency, which is similar to you in your physical condition. A final limitation is that they have to work and exist as a multiple, that is, for every one of you, for instance, there are four to five of them.

ME: *But we can incarnate in up to twelve physical vehicles at the same time! (I had received this in a previous short meditation. It was another use of the number twelve).*

SE2: That is true in your case, but I have not worked in the same way as your Source Entity. Also, whereas you may incarnate in twelve separate vehicles in as many different dimensions or universes, they are restricted to being in the same universe and in the same locale. Even more restricting is the fact that they must work together to experience their experiences and work towards their evolution as a group, even though they are not what you would call a "group soul."

ME: *So are they spread out into different civilizations: a group here, a group there, some populating a planet, some populating a galaxy. Does one group communicate with another group who has decided to exist in another neighboring planet, solar system or galaxy?*

SE2: A lot of questions in one sentence.

ME: *Sorry.*

SE2: First, let me give you a bit more of the picture in this environment. Although in the physical sense it is equivalent in volume to the first, it is not equivalent in dimensionality, which also affects the physical. Do I make sense here as this may seem like nonsense to you?

ME: Carry on; I think I know what you mean.

SE2: You may, but I will explain for the wider audience. You are fortunate to have a multi-dimensional multiverse to work with; the beings in my second environment do not. As a result, they do not have access to the physical levels that are above the physical levels where you currently exist. Thus, in effect they are limited to the physicality of the environment they exist within. They cannot go above or below it. I know you can't go below the level that you are physically. You are at rock bottom, but you can go above. I will repeat, those in environment one can't do either. You are fortunate in this way.

ME: So they are captive in a certain environmental existence—one that you have created, one that they must work with.

SE2: Yes, that's the deal.

ME: O.K., let's move on. Can I get back to what they have achieved as a civilization?

SE2: Of course. You have to recognize though that the clues that you use in your physical existence to define a civilization and what it needs to do to be , is entirely different to what this race would consider civilization.

ME: How do you mean?

SE2: You may consider some of the actions they take to be that of an underdeveloped world.

ME: Are you trying to tell me that they are savages?

SE2: No they are not, at least not in the sense that you think. You see, their civilization is very, very basic. They are limited to a level of frequency that you would call energetic, but they would consider it physical.

ME: Why would they consider it physical if we consider it energetic?

53

SE2: Because they have adopted a form that is impervious to them—that is, they can feel total resistance to their surroundings, themselves, and between themselves. I can see that you are frowning; you are thinking that this means that they are no different than you in your environment, am I correct?

ME: *You are correct. I would have thought that they would need to be incarnate to be "physical."*

SE2: Physicality is an expectation that you have that is based upon your current level of experience. You have a similar level of expectation for the registration and recognition of events that are individual and personal to the entity and its surroundings. You call it "time." Know this: everything in this second environment is energetic but has what you would call a "physical" aspect to it. This is not to say that these entities are subject to the same levels of limitation that you are; they are not. They can create structures in/on the areas that they focus on— that is, where in their universe they tend to be or like to be when they are together in groups made up of groups where they experience existence. Remember that is multiples of the groups of four or five that they are part of in their sphere of evolution and experience. They can use these structures for recreation, learning, or sharing of experiences. The area where you may call them uncivilized comes into play when one or two of the group, or even a whole group, are not progressing. In this instance, they are "cast outside" the group or groups that are at the same evolutionary or experience level. They are cast out to fend for themselves; they are not let back into the group or groups.

ME: *You say they are cast out! Is this forever?*

SE2: Yes, it is. Although they may form groups that are made up of other cast-outs.

ME: *Hold on. I have just got a grip on what you are saying here. You have entities that are cast out of their prime*

54

evolutionary environment simply because they are not considered to be progressing as well as some or all the others within a group. Is this correct?

SE2: Yes.

ME: That's not very spiritual, is it? I mean it's not very loving! It's not loving the entities that you have created. In fact, from where I am sitting, it looks and feels very draconian to me.

SE: This is one of the things that you will have to get used to when dealing with the other Source Entities. That is, they may and will use very different methods of progression and evolution than those which are experiencing in my environment.

ME: O.K., sorry. I was expecting to see everything that comes from the Origin as being in love and light and full of fluffy pink bunnies.

SE2: I see where you are coming from now. Do you want me to filter my communication with you and only give you that which falls within the category that you expect?

ME: No, no. That would not give the correct picture to the seekers of true truth.

SE2: O.K., let me explain this "casting out" process in a different way as I can see that this has disturbed you significantly.

ME: Go ahead.

SE2: Perhaps you have read something into the use of the word "cast out" that is not intentional.

ME: Possibly, you do have to work with my very limited communication abilities.

SE2: Yes, I am finding it a challenge. Nevertheless, I will continue with my communication with you. Those entities that are cast out leave the group both at the request of the group and under their own volition. Both the group and the entity not progressing realize that the best thing for both parties is to become separate. This allows them both to progress at their own rate. It is a

55

most efficient method. You must understand this in a different way; in your multiverse, you are singular in your evolution. You both succeed and are succeeded by entities that are slower and faster than you in your evolutionary progression. Your evolution is personal. You wish well of those who you pass and offer good luck to those who pass you. This is the way of your multiverse. It is similar in mine, only the entities in this particular environment operate in groups. Let me make something else also clear. The "cast out" process is also used on those entities that appear to outgrow their group. This is done so that they can find a group that is similar in progression to their own although as you can imagine, this is a rarer occurrence since the main reason for being in the group is to progress as a group and not as a singular entity.

ME: *You said that they were cast out forever. What do you mean by this statement then?*

SE2: They will never be able to return to the group that they have left, for the group has either outgrown them, or they have outgrown the group.

In the instance that they have out grown the group, they have a limited opportunity for further progression in the short term since one of the first things they have to do is find a new group, which as I stated earlier is hard to do because they are far and few between. They cannot progress without a group, so they must spend the rest of their time as cast outs looking for a group that is in a similar level of progression to them. Once they have established a group that fits the bill, they have to negotiate to be allowed to enter the group.

ME: *Why do they have to negotiate?*

SE2: Because in some instances they may actually reduce the progression level of the group they are joining in some small way, or they may actually increase the progression. As you can imagine, finding a group that is exactly the same in terms of their "individual progression level" as a cast out is difficult. In terms of an entity that is cast out because of lack of progression, finding a new group to work with is probably harder, especially if the entity is very slow in progression. In this instance the entity can wander the environment "group less" for millennia (in your terms). The best opportunity in this instance is creating a new group by working with other entities in a similar position. However, as previously noted, there will be a level of negotiation that goes on here as well, as one of the entities will undoubtedly be a faster "progressor" than the other, even if the progression is very minor in comparison. Joining together these two temporarily singular entities will result in one of them reducing its progression level to a point that is the mean of the two entities. This means that the lower level entity benefits in the collaboration as its level will increase creating a level of dependency between the two. Hence, the correct and formal formation of a new and recognizable group, a group of two, one that will attract other singular entities and, therefore, grow to the optimal size for the group's opportunity to progress in its evolution. So as you can see, being outcast is not such a big issue. It is a natural process of group evolution, one that is standard within this environment.

ME: *A few moments ago in this dialogue you mentioned groups of groups. Does this mean that groups can get together for evolutionary purposes?*

SE2: Yes, of course. This is one of the primary functions of progression. Groups of similar progression levels can cluster together in just the same way as single entities cluster together to form a single group. This allows them to both share group evolutionary experiences and to work on opportunities that present themselves by allowing intergroup dynamics to take place.

ME: *What kind of intergroup dynamics?*

SE2: There are three main types of inter-group dynamics. The first type is the interaction as groups between groups with the groups working and acting as if they are one entity, which is, indeed, what they should be. The second type is two or more groups working together by allowing the single entities that make up the groups to move from one group to another at will. The groups appear to merge at the point of interaction, and doubling or trebling in size is observed whilst the dynamic is being worked on. This allows a sharing of individual experience outside the entities' normal group. The third interaction is a mixture of the two mentioned above. That is, three, four, or more groups interact both on a group basis and an individual entity basis together with the single entities moving between one or more groups outside their own main group on a regular basis. In this last interaction, a lot of evolutionary opportunities can be progressed as all the groups seem to lose their individual group identity at one point or another with completely new groups being formed at times. In this instance, both group and individual entity interaction within different group interactions happen all at the same time, which gives the visual appearance of an undulating mass of entity movement resulting in the form and the formless, the timed and the timeless, the frequency and frequency-less, the dimension and dimensionless intermingling and entwining. It is beautiful to watch.

ME: *It strikes me that what you have just described could also be used to described what happens on our planet, Earth, as we have interaction between individuals, families, local communities, countries, and civilizations, together with migration between them all.*

SE2: To some extent, yes, but in comparison to my group interaction and dynamics, your communities, countries, civilizations, etc., are one-dimensional (1D).

ME: *But we are three-dimensional.*

SE2: Yes, but you would appear one-dimensional comparatively speaking.

ME: *What do you mean one-dimensional?*

SE2: As they are at a different base dimension and frequency to you, they are naturally more expansive even though they have physicality between themselves. So, by referring to you (the human race) as being one-dimensional, I am trying to illustrate your limitations in comparison to theirs. For example, if they were to present themselves into your universe, galaxy, dimension, and frequency, you would not be able to detect them even with your sensing machines because your machines are not calibrated to sense the essence of their physicality, which to you is not physical.

Environment 3—An Environment for Change

ME: *I would like to talk about the third environment you have created. How is this different than the first two?*

SE2: Environment 1 is closed to all but those entities that exist within it. As previously stated, they have the same abilities ("power" if you want to call it that) as I do. They cannot return to their Source, me.

Environment 2 has one dimension and one frequency, and although the entities can return to me at any time, they must work and evolve in groups or groups of groups. They exist in a finer density than humankind.

59

Environment 3 is different again. It is what you call "fluidic" in nature.

ME: *You mean it's full of water or a liquid of some sort?*

SE2: No, no. By fluidic I mean that it is constantly changing.

ME: *In what way does it constantly change? Is it in dimension? Is it in frequency? Is it in physicality?*

SE2: Nearly, in fact, it changes in a way that you will have difficulty understanding.

ME: *Try me.*

SE2: O.K. It changes in rotational attractivity. I can see that you are frowning again.

ME: *I am a bit as I am trying to work out what that may mean. Can you describe it in layman's terms, please?*

SE2: Everything in this environment has a force that I call "rotational attractivity;" you might call it gravity, but it is not. In this instance, rotational attractivity is the random function that occurs in this environment that causes an entity to slip uncontrollably from one dimension or frequency to another at a specific point in its existence as a result of its natural attractivity to that dimension or frequency. By rotational attractivity, I mean that the dimensions above and below the position of the entity concerned have a rotational component that is peculiar to a certain frequency or dimension. You might call it the "speed of the energetic components" that makeup the entity.

ME: *How can rotation be described as speed?*

SE2: The associated energetic components move about and around each other. In some instances the configuration of these energies matches another environmental condition better than its current one so it is, therefore, attracted to it. If the level of attraction is compatible with enough of the energetic components of the entity concerned, it modifies the remaining components and slips into the next dimensional/frequency-based environment, that is, the one that it has been attracted to.

60

ME: *That must be a very difficult way to live.*

SE2: Why?

ME: *Because the entity that slips from one, shall I say "rotational environment" to another would have to start all over again every time it changes environments.*

SE2: You are thinking in terms of your own dimension and frequency again. The entities that exist in the third environment know when they are close to being moved from one type of rotational environment to another. As a result they prepare themselves for the change and work out/clear up all that they have started in their current environment. What's more, as they become more and more aligned to their next rotational existence, they get a feel of what limitations or abilities they will have. As a result and to a certain degree, they can plan ahead what they can achieve evolution-wise before they make the change.

ME: *But it must be like moving and losing all of your possessions, your job, and your house at the same time on a frequent basis.*

SE2: Not quite, for these entities don't need to work to sustain themselves. They don't need to buy food or clothing or shelter of any sort. They exist in an ever-changing environment and, as a result, they need to be independent of such restrictions.

ME: *So do they work by themselves, or do they work in groups like the entities in the second environment?*

SE2: They work on themselves for themselves, but they can and do work together with other entities for mutual advancement if they so desire. But of course, this generally only lasts for the duration that either one of them is in that rotational environment.

ME: *Can one entity follow another entity to another rotational environment?*

SE2: No, not willingly, but they can continue to work together if they detect each other later. As you can imagine, the chances of this happening is limited.

ME: *But not impossible I take it.*

SE2: No it is not impossible, but it is unlikely, especially since most of the entities plan a piece of work that is generally small enough to be contained in the shortest of existences within their current rotational environment.

ME: *So how would an entity know how long it has and how would it know if another entity had enough time left in their environment to make a partnership work and work to a successful conclusion?*

SE2: Each entity has an energetic signature that is relevant to its current rotational environment and the one that it will be slipping into. Consider it like an hour glass with sand running from one side of the glass bubble to the other through the small piece of glass that connects them. The top side of the glass is where they are now and the bottom side is where they are being attracted to next. It is this signature that every entity can sense in terms of the current rotational environment; it's just that they can't tell where their next environment will be.

ME: *So if I was an entity in this environment, how would I sense the longevity of the entity next to me.*

SE2: You would just know. I can see that statement is not enough for you.

ME: *No. You mentioned the hour glass as an example, but this was an example of an energetic signature. An entity must have some sort of representation, for instance, visual that makes fast recognition of longevity.*

SE2: Yes, there is. The best way to describe it in terms that you can understand in the physical is to say that they have a color associated with the length of time they have left in their current environment. Of course, there are a lot more colors available than those in your visible spectrum, but a good facsimile would be the change in color from the infrared to the ultraviolet. As an accurate example, it is inadequate but will do for now.

ME: *Simplistically speaking then, they change from red to blue, or from white to black.*

SE2: If this helps you understand, then that will do.

ME: *What do the entities in Environment 3 work on to help them evolve, and do they have enough of them grouped together to create a civilization?*

SE2: I can see that you are enthralled with the need to be civilized in a way that you can recognize in the physical. No, don't answer. It is written all over your face, so to speak. I am told by your Source Entity that this is a common desire, one that you all have difficulty moving away from.

Mmm, I will have to enlighten you in the simple general rules that I ask my creations to work within:

- Evolve through experimentation and experience.
- Work together where necessary.
- Do not create anything that could be detrimental to yourself or others.
- Be of service (you also have this rule to work with).
- Do not intentionally harm another.
- It is the quality of experience that counts, not how fast you experience the experience.

ME: *That last rule is a really good one. It is one that we should adopt in our physical existence.*

SE2: If you could all embrace it, you would all benefit greatly. But, let's get back to answering your questions.

My creations in the third environment are independent of the need to coalesce to exist, purely because they are not located in one place only. As with all of my creations in all of my environments, they are creatures of the universe they exist within and as such have access to all of it without exception. The only limitations they

63

have in this sense are those that they place on themselves as part of their evolutionary plans. If enough of them are in a specific environment long enough to find that their working together in a large group is to the advantage of all, then they will group together; otherwise, they will limit their interaction to ones or twos. There will never be a group large enough to create a civilization in the sense that you know, for it is not a requirement for evolution as it is with you. In terms of what they work on, you would not understand most of it. Suffice to say, they experience things that can only be experienced by continuous change of environment and the level of attractivity it has with them.

Environment 4—An Environment Aware of Its Own Existence

ME: *O.K., tell me about the fourth and final environment that you created. What limitations did you put on this universe?*

SE2: The fourth environment was given the opportunity to evolve on its own. That is, I did not personally create any entities specifically to exist within this environment, which is, of course, a different strategy than the one used in the creation of the other environments.

ME: *Hang on. Are you saying that the environment evolved on its own and created its own entities?*

SE2: In a word, yes, although that is not specifically how it happened. The environment itself was created and given the opportunity to become aware on its own in its own time, so to speak. It was, in essence, like me: energy given sentience/individuality whereas the other environments are just that, environments with no sentience. The sentience is given to the entities I created specifically to exist within that environment.

Environment 4 was given the gift of individuality and the opportunity to evolve in its own right.

ME: *I'm getting the impression that you copied, for want of a better word, the Origin in this instance. The Origin gave the twelve Source Entities, you, part of its volume to give you individuality and an opportunity to evolve in your own way. In Environment 4's case, you gave it the same opportunity that the Origin gave to you, some of your own volume and the means to become aware of self and, therefore, gain a level of sentience.*

SE2: Correct. It is a very interesting project and one that has borne much fruit from an evolutionary perspective.

ME: *So how did you advise Environment 4 on its task in existence?*

SE2: The same way the Origin gave me my set of rules to work within. In fact, they are identical. This was the best way to proceed in this instance.

ME: *How long did it take Environment 4 to gain awareness?*

SE2: You are always referring to time; your Source Entity warned me about this trait and said that it is one of your biggest limitations.

ME: *Sorry, but it is one of the methods that humankind in my Source Entities' multiverse uses to differentiate between the advent of an number of events and their relationship to each other. It is also a datum that the readers of this text will use as a tool to try to understand the details of what we are discussing.*

SE2: If it makes things easy for you, then I will use it although time is a non-concept. It means nothing.

ME: *O.K., I understand.*

SE2: Yes, I believe you do at a deep down fundamental level—the level that is the real you, the energetic you, so let's move on. In creating Environment 4 in this way, I gave it essence of "me." In some respects, this helped it on its way to awareness. As a result it established its awareness quite quickly. In your metric of time, this would be about a billion years. I also noticed that the awareness coalesced in one area of denser energy where the energy distribution of the environment was irregular or uneven. In fact, the environment became aware in a type of energy that was similar in make-up.

ME: *I have just received an image of a dark cloud of energy within the bubble of Environment 4—that dark cloud being the energy that gained awareness first. This darker energy is still distributed throughout the volume that is Environment 4. It is just that this area was denser and thus ended up at the center of awareness.*

SE2: Good, that is correct. The rest of the environment also gained awareness but at a slower pace. Consider it like when you wake up from being asleep. At first you are aware of just your thoughts, and then you start to feel certain parts of your body, some before others. Finally you are in full awareness of your body, and you move your limbs at will without preconceived thought. This is exactly how Environment 4 became aware. First, it was in the center of the dark energy cloud. Then as awareness of self spread, it became more expansive and started to include the rest of the dark energy spread throughout the environmental bubble. Eventually it also included the other energies that are also present, making it a complete environmental entity in its own right— fully aware of its existence, its composition, its location, and its abilities.

ME: *How could it be aware of its abilities so early in its existence?*

SE2: As I stated before, it had essence of me, and as a result of its growing awareness, it also gained knowledge of its personal attributes and abilities. Although at this point in its existence they were fairly rudimentary, they were enough to kick-start the higher level functions of an entity that was not limited in its creative ability within the confines of what I had given it. In fact, it very quickly established what it could and couldn't do. The abilities that it couldn't perform were a function of its ability to control and work with the energies that formed its volume so to speak. So as it gained more and more understanding of self it gained more and more experience, and as a result, it expanded its creative abilities.

ME: *So it grew in capability as it increased in awareness.*

SE2: Correct. When it reached a point where it realized that it was part of a much larger entity, and, therefore, started to probe its boundaries, I decided to make my presence known and advise Environment 4 on its role in life, as it were.

ME: *So at this point you were able to work with Environment 4 because it was at a level of awareness that allowed it to understand what you were conveying.*

SE2: Yes. It needed to be at this point for a couple of reasons. First, it had to have enough awareness to allow a robust level of understanding, and second, it had to be young enough not to question its position in the universe and go off at a tangent to what I wanted to achieve.

ME: *Are you suggesting that there is an optimal time period for intervention and presentation of advice on an entity's role in existence?*

SE2: Absolutely. Know this. If an entity is briefed on its role in existence too early in its awakening, that time during which it is becoming what it is, then it will not fully appreciate what you are telling it and will not give it the level of importance that it deserves. If on the other hand you wait too long in the awakening process, the entity develops too much independence, is likely to question the need for the role it is given, and is inclined to rebel. Although on the face of it, letting an entity experience this would be an interesting experiment to perform and observe, it is not on my agenda for evolutionary experience at this present point in my existence.

ME: *I have to admit I am a little bit surprised that an entity needs to be coached in this way and that there is an optimal time period in which it has to (must) be done. I would have given an entity of this size and ability more credibility.*

SE2: (Pause) Forgive me. I have just tapped into your memory to understand more about you and your environment. Are you O.K. with this?

ME: *Yes.*

SE2: Good, for it will help me answer your questions better. Consider a human child. If you give it too much leeway, it will not respect you. If you are too hard on it, it will consider you a tyrant. Both responses result in it holding you in contempt. This is the same for any entity. No matter how expansive and powerful it is, it is still immature. It has experienced nothing, it has learnt nothing, it has not begun its evolution, and it has no morals or understanding of what is the right thing to do and what is detrimental. Notice that I didn't say "wrong thing," for there is no wrong thing that can be done as everything is experience and evolution.

ME: *So what you are saying is that even though an entity may be as big as the fourth environment, it is still juvenile in nature.*

SE2: In a nutshell, yes, but don't get me wrong. The level of juvenility is completely different to what you expect and experience in your physical human existence as it would still be considered a god even by the most evolved entity within your universe.

ME: *O.K., now I think I understand the need to be accurate in the point of intervention of the awakening of a new entity.*

SE2: I have one further thing to add. The point of intervention is also important because of the ability of the entity to absorb the information that it is going to be given. This is additional to its briefing on its role in existence.

ME: *What information do you give it?*

SE2: In Environment 4's instance, a portion of the learning that I have gained during my existence—just enough to give it a head start. I could have left it totally on its own, but that would not have been conducive to my plan. And that plan was that Environment 4 had essence of "me." In the case of other entities, I give them enough memory-based information to back up the briefing I give them. In this way they understand fully what I ask of them and are able to "hit the ground running," as you would say.

ME: *So if I get this correctly, the point of intervention is a point in the early existence of the entity where it has not yet accrued its own knowledge base and as a result cannot, therefore, reject the information that you give it since it would be comparing the two sets of information all of the time.*

SE2: Correct. The memories that I implant need to be accepted as its own, and this cannot be done after it starts to accrue its own memories.

ME: *O.K., can we move on a bit?*

SE2: Of course.

ME: *From what I can see, the fourth environment is a unique experiment. I mean, giving a whole universe sentience—that's quite a step.*

SE2: It's not as unique as you think. All I have done in this instance is give the energy that I call the fourth environment the essence of "me" and the opportunity to create on its own. This has been done in preference to my creation of an environment and then populating it with other smaller entities. Even with this second scenario the environment itself will at some point in its existence accrue a certain level of awareness. This is normal and to be expected, for all energy has the ability to gain awareness given enough time to stabilize, attract like energies, and grow in volume.

ME: *So are you saying that all energy can be sentient in some way, shape, or form?*

SE2: In my plan, yes, and your own Source Entity has allowed your universe to have a certain level of awareness. It's just that you don't recognize it in your current state. The only thing you need to understand is this: environments that evolve awareness and sentience are still part of the greater whole—in this instance, one of the other Source Entities or me, which are also part of the wider whole of the Origin. They never become FULLY individual to the point of separation from the originating entity. The small level of individuality that the environment gains as a result of elevating itself up to sentient status is merely localized to the energy that I or any of the other Source Entities have separated from our selves. It is a sub-section of our energy, and as a result is separate in function but whole in application. I do not lose wholeness as a result of separation. Giving an environment individuality does not reduce my wholeness for it is a process similar to what I use to create the smaller entities who populate the other environments I have created.

I can see that you are frowning.

The environments are like my major organs, and the smaller entities are like the cells that make up those organs. Consider it like one of your own organs—say your brain. You think that your sentience, your intellect, your individuality is centrally located in the organ you call the brain. This is not the case. In reality that part of you that is energetic is the real you, and the part that is associated with this physical vehicle is a small part of the real you. However, that part of you is associated with the whole of the physical body and not just the brain; it's just that you credit the brain with the power of individual thought when, in actuality, individual thought comes from the energetic. If you gave yourself the time to listen to the rest of your body's components, you would notice that they all have a level of intelligence. They all have individual function. Currently you recognize the personality of physical self as being the "person." You center the mind at the brain while actually the mind is the *whole* of you, physical and energetic, even though the physical is transient.

It is the ability to recognize that the sum of the functions of the individual parts create the self. That gives an entity the understanding of the evolutionary advantage available by the creation of smaller parts of itself within itself that gives them individuality and the ability to evolve as individuals. In essence, I become more as a result of giving a part of myself individuality because personal energy given individuality remains a solid part of the whole. Your liver is individual but part of the whole. Your heart is individual but part of the whole. Your pancreas is individual but part of the whole, and your lungs are individual but part of the whole. Your physical body is an excellent example of what I describe; it is a microcosm of the macrocosm.

So to simplify: giving a volume of energy the size of a universal environment individuality and sentience is no different to giving an entity of your volume of energy individuality. The subdivision of energy within energy and giving it individuality does not result in a reduction of size of the original entity. It remains part of the whole. Does this explain this concept for you?

ME: *Yes, it does. Thank you.*

Earlier in this dialogue we talked about the limitations you placed on the environments you created. What other limitations did you enforce on Environment 4?

SE2: The fourth environment was also limited in physicality. By this I mean that the environment is purely energetic, and it is not possible for the entities that the environment created and that exist within it to affect each other in any way like you can, such as by touch or feel. They are like gasses mixing together but not in a way that creates a new gas.

ME: *How do you mean?*

SE2: In the multiverse that you are part of, you can mix materials together to get what you call alloys. This you do with varying levels of ease/difficulty. You even have a gas alloy that you call air although it is made up of many constituent parts and is not a true alloy in the sense of harder materials, such as bronze or aluminium. Air is a naturally occurring alloy and is not the product of fusing together materials at the atomic level to create the new material. Air is actually a good example of the way different entities interact at the physical level without merging together to create a new entity.

ME: *Can you explain this a bit further?*

SE2: Yes of course. The entities in this environment are purely energetic. As a result, they are of a higher frequency than your physical vehicles. They all resonate in a different way. The way that they resonate is specific to each of them as individuals; as a result, they are not able to increase or decrease their frequency to a level where they are in synchronicity with another entity.

ME: *So you could say that they have their own signature.*

SE2: No, individual entity signature and resonant frequency are different things in this environment although I can see where you are coming from. This can and does work well in your home environment. However, this is not the case in this environment as the limitations imposed upon it dictate that this is not possible. An entity's resonant frequency is a product of its basic makeup. Each individual entity has a unique resonant frequency, but this is not what is used to distinguish themselves one from another, for they are not aware of their own frequency as such. They use a method of pulsing—what you call "light".

ME: *Oh, that's interesting. We can see light with our physical eyes.*

SE2: But you wouldn't be able to see *this* light, for it is of a completely different nature. You have light at two ends of your physical visible spectrum, do you not?

ME: *Yes, we call it ultraviolet and infrared.*

SE2: And you cannot see any of their wavelengths with your physical eyes.

ME: *No, but we can detect it with our instruments. We can also see infrared light if we use the view finder or display of a digital camera, as the couple charge devices (CCD Array) that the camera uses to detect the different light frequencies and luminance levels are sensitive to wavelengths that we cannot see with our physical eyes but are nevertheless presented back to the observer via the digital camera's screen. It is detected, so it is interpreted and displayed.*

SE2: Well, if you had a CCD array that was sensitive to frequencies above 200,000 of what you call nano-meters, you might be able to detect the light that the entities in Environment 4 use to differentiate one another.

ME: *Do they use this high frequency light as a language?*

SE2: They can but choose not to, for that is a method of communication that is as inefficient as the pushing air across that part of your body that you call the vocal cords to create a different frequency of that air, resulting in different sounds you call "words"—a most inefficient method of communication if I have ever experienced

73

one. The use of light to communicate is just as inefficient.

ME: *But it would travel at the speed of light!*

SE2: The speed of light is variable and not the constant that you think it is, for it is dependent upon the overlying frequency of its environment or universe.

ME: *How can this be? I thought that light is one of the physical constants that we can rely on.*

SE2: Is light not based upon a particle, the photon?

ME: *Yes.*

SE2: Does it not have weight and a resonant frequency as a particle?

ME: *You would have to ask a physicist on that one, but I guess that it does.*

SE2: Well, the answer is that it does and as a result of this, it is easily affected by the frequentic changes within its environment. It is also affected by what you call "gravity" and "magnetic fields."

ME: *I have just received information to suggest that this causes distortion in the information that is transmitted using light.*

SE2: Well done! Yes, it does. Also, the entities within Environment 4 are by their very nature quite a distance apart physically and spatially with some being many billions of what you call "light years away." As a result of this, they need a method of communication that isn't limited by physical constraints, such as distance, speed, weight, and frequency.

ME: *So what do they use? Telepathy?*

SE2: A form of telepathy, yes, although they are capable of much more than communication based upon thought. This is because they are still part of Environment 4 and do not have full independence or singularity.

ME: *I am having difficulty understanding what you are transmitting to me. I know that you have just sent me the answer, but I have nothing to compare it with. In fact, just thinking about what to compare it with is making me very tired.*

SE2: Yes, I understand. That is because you are trying to stretch your perception beyond me and communicate directly with that part of the fourth environment that is occupied with these entities. The communication medium that you are receiving would be best described as similar to your "surround sound" but for another medium, not for sound, for this is also slow.

At this point I needed to break off for a rest as the concentration was intense. I returned a couple of hours later with renewed vigor.

ME: Ah, I get it now. They have many channels of communication, and they use the environment itself as the basis for that communication. This has the effect of a single entity talking to itself. They, therefore, don't communicate as single entities when they communicate. They communicate as a whole. They are the environment.

SE2: Good, good. Now you are aligned with the appropriate frequency to receive higher levels of information— information that is totally alien to you.

ME: I also get the impression that all of the entities that populate the four environments you have created are energetic in nature and do not need to exist in the presence of a planet, star, or any other larger body?

SE2: As you see it, the physical body is a peculiarity of your universe. In general, the projection of self to such depths of frequency is not a prerequisite for progressing evolution. As you rightly noted, all my entities are energy-based all of the time, and the entities that Environment 4 created are no exception to this. In fact, I have one thing to note. None of my entities have experienced existence at the frequencies you have. In this you are unique, even within your own universe, for other physical entities are a much higher frequency.

ME: *Do the entities in Environment 4 have any planets to live on?*

SE2: No, they live in free space so to speak. They have no need for a focal point within which to exist, for they already have one—the environment that created them.

ME: *I would find it hard to interact with them as most of our interaction in the physical relies on the ability to see, touch, and hear each other. From what you have explained to me, they are not able to do or use any of these senses.*

SE2: And they would find it difficult to use them as well. Remember, these entities are the product of the individual thought of an environment, not me and as a result they are subject to variation upon what would be expected from the short sortie you have made into the other three environments I created. The entities in the fourth environment are constrained by their physicality not their "physicalness," their makeup, which is to you energetic in nature. They are able to work with each other and the environment that created them. They are able to maintain their individuality whilst being blending together, they can communicate in a most efficient and instantaneous manner, they are the children of one of my greater creations and of this I am pleased.

I suddenly sensed that this was the end of my communication with Source Entity 2. It was gone from my mind, and I felt empty, I felt that I could function again without feeling that the walls were closing in around me—a feeling that must have been due to the sheer volume of information that I was receiving and having to filter down to text in my computer. This was my first communication with another Source Entity— a Source Entity that was not my creator. Although we had discussed its work and achievements over the last few weeks, I felt that I hadn't even scratched the surface, that I had gained nothing. I found myself asking the age-old question of whether or not it was all worthwhile when my own Source Entity cut in.

SE: You are disappointed.

ME: *I expected to get more information than this. I expected to get down to the sort of level where I could ask what kind of civilizations were in SE2's environments, what they have achieved, what they have created, even what car they drive* (if they had a car).

SE: You would never be able to assimilate that level of data from a foreign Source Entity. Indeed, it is not possible to go to that depth with me and some of my other groups of entities, for there is simply too much detail. Consider how you would explain 21st century technology and life to a 17th century person. You couldn't do that in any detail that would be understandable simply because the language is not there, and language /understanding is the limiting factor here. Let me tell you this. These limited dialogues that you have with me, my peers, and, indeed, the Origin are enough to whet the appetite of any seeker of truth. They are by their very nature an overview of what is out there in the greater reality, and an overview is all that mankind in its current state can cope with right now. Do not be disappointed, my friend, for you break new ground. Enough is enough, and the detail in these short dialogues is more than enough to be getting on with. You will be communicating with Source Entity Three next, and you will need to shift your energies to a different level than you have currently experienced to achieve communication. For this you will need to rest and purify yourself, for SE3 is pure of heart and energy.

Chapter 3

Source Entity Three

I have to admit that at this point in the game I am feeling a little worried. I feel that the information that I have already received as a result of my communications with the first two Source Entities is very high level and not of enough detail to be of importance. I also feel that it is diverse enough to cover most of what I could possibly expect. In fact, I can't possibly think what would come out of dialogue with the other Source Entities that would be enough to create a robust piece of work that is of interest to the spiritual public. It is a real dichotomy. The feeling is a little bit akin to writer's block, except that it is "channeler's block," or is it? It could be that the task at hand is so large that I am daunted by it to the point of inactivity, of mental seizure, of doubt. I am also worried that the details that I have taken down are the result of a vivid imagination, that I am not in contact with other Source Entities, and that I am, in effect, just talking to myself. As I type these words, my fears are being put to one side specifically because now I feel that I have already made a mental link with Source Entity Three (SE3) to the point where I have a mental image of what it looks like. Also, my own Source Entity is here with me and has a few words of comfort and help.

ME: *I feel that I can't carry on with this, that I can't conjure up enough diversity of information to justify the goal of having a chapter on each Source Entity.*

SE: Be calm. It does not matter how many words you receive on each Source Entity. What matters is that you contact them, and you open your heart to them. You are thinking that you have to create the text yourself and that you can't possibly have enough diversity of creative

79

thought to create new dialogue of the length you have already achieved. This is your ego talking to you. You will be given the information; you will not have to invent it. Your fears are borne out of self-created objectives. Your personal objectives are not important. What will be, will be. Remember what one of your old managers said to you once: bite your elephant in bite-size chunks. You don't have to do it all in one go. There are no time constraints. There are no limitations.

The information is and must be high level. As I stated at the end of our dialogue with Source Entity Two, you can't possibly go down to the minute detail that you wish. You simply don't have enough capacity in your current physical state, and your readers would not appreciate this level of detail either. You are more likely to bore the pants off them!

I was about to say that this is a bit of a backward step for you, but I have just looked into your mind and now understand what the issue is. It is not fear of being able to meet your objective of 12,000 words per Source Entity or your worry about the information being diverse enough to be credible.

ME: *So what is it then?*

SE: You are trying to access too much at the same time. As a result, you don't know which way to look first. You are like a deer in the headlights of a car. No, wait a minute. You are accessing ALL the Source Entities at the same time, and you are close to information overload. No wonder you are feeling like you can't do anything. You are full to the point of bursting. Re-calibrate your awareness to me and Source Entity Three only. This will help.

Initial Contact with Source Entity Three—Blissful!

I took the advice of my Source Entity. I mentally told myself that I would only receive information from my own Source Entity and Source Entity Three. The effect was remarkable. I suddenly felt lighter, cleaner, open. All of my fears about what I was doing left me, and the fog cleared from my mind. I must be careful not to open myself too much again, or I must train myself to accept the increase in information.

At this point I found myself logging into Source Entity Three. Again I saw the image of it. I approached it from the perspective of the Origin, looking inward and downward to see its appearance and location within the Origin. The initial impression I received was that of an amorphous white ball that undulated. It felt warm, comforting, even welcoming. It was a delight to be in its presence. What's more it was pleased to sense me and invited me inside itself. It felt pure. It was pure. It was pure of heart, just like my Source Entity told me. I was in a state of bliss, one I had not experienced in communications with my own Source Entity. I opened a dialogue.

ME: *Wow, it feels totally euphoric! It's a very heady feeling. Why is this?*

SE3: What you are feeling is the result of the work that I am doing. Within your own Source Entity's environments, you are allowed to experience different levels of "-ivity."

ME: *-ivity?*

SE3: -ivity. You see them in two basic ways though: positivity and negativity. In my experiment and in all of the environments that I have created, there is no such thing as negativity. I can see that you are about to ask a question.

ME: *Yes, my own Source Entity says there is no such thing as a negative experience. There is only experience.*

81

SE3: Yes, that is true, but in my environments there can be no experience that can be classified as bad, detrimental, or horrible. Everything is delightful; every entity works in harmony in everything it does.

ME: *I find this a bit hard to take on-board. How can everything be done in a state of bliss?*

SE3: In comparison with your current existence, everything in the Origin's multiverse is experienced in a state of bliss. That which is not in bliss is generally of such a low frequency that it is unbearable.

ME: *Are you suggesting that bliss is a state of frequency?*

SE3: No, but it is a component part of it. An entity that is in a state of bliss is usually of a high frequency.

ME: *So why would you want to create a universe where its entities are only able to experience positive blissful things?*

SE3: Quite simply, to see what happens. One of the things you will notice in your dialogues with the Source Entities is that each of us is doing things its way. Sometimes there is an overlap in what we do, and sometimes we are poles, even multiverses, apart. Where we overlap, we compare and contrast what we did and how we arrived at the condition, what the route was, what the circumstances were, and what the incumbent entity's contribution was that resulted in that end result. Where we do not overlap, we share our learning and add it to the total reservoir of evolutionary data that we create. Why shouldn't I have an experiment where every entity that exists within an environment is in blissful harmony?

ME: *Well, I would consider that it limits the experience opportunity.*

SE3: It does, and that is the point.

Let me make it easier for you. Although you would think that you are limiting the evolutionary opportunities of an entity or environment by initiating such limitations, what you are actually doing is opening up an opportunity to focus on an aspect of existence to a greater depth of detail. To some extent, this is what you are doing now in your physical, low frequency existence. The objective of the experience and resultant evolutionary opportunity is not just in the quantity of things that you experience, it is also in the quality of what you experience. To achieve this, you must limit your options. To put it in a nutshell, as you might say, the entities in my environments are to experience existence in a state of bliss or positivity in every which way they can and as much as they can.

ME: *My own Source Entity said that you are "Pure of Heart." I have an understanding of what that means from my own sense, but can you tell me what your understanding is?*

SE3:   Simply put, it is the way I do business in my environments. What do I mean by this?

ME: *I don't know. Maybe it is that you do not stray off the beaten track. You stick to your strategy that you cannot be corrupted in any way by any of the things that your creations do, and you expect the same from your creations.*

SE3:   Good try. In my instance, being pure of heart is that I only have the best intentions in mind and only want the best for my creations and their experiences. That is why I limited their environment to the higher frequency levels: those levels that result in the condition you call "bliss."

ME: *What does it feel like to live continually in this bliss state that you have created for your creations?*

SE3:   I can only explain it from your perspective.

It would be like being in a continuous state of well-being, good cheer, and good humor. You would not have any ailments, worries, or concerns. Everything is understood and understandable. Everything is achieved and achievable. Anything that the individual does is for the good of all, including the environment. Nothing is detrimental. Nothing detrimental can be or is desired to be done. No one does anything just for self. Everything is done in love and light.

ME: *Whilst you were describing this, I started to experience it. I felt like I was in a cloud of light that I was free of any restrictions and constraints. I felt FREE in every sense of the word.*

SE3: Even though my entities are constrained to only experiencing the bliss state, the level of freedom from your perspective is infinite.

ME: *It felt like I was everywhere all at the same time—in communication with all things and everything all at the same time. Being restricted to the bliss state does not seem like a restriction to me. It seems like a delight, an honor, something to be cherished.*

SE3: Ah. You have hit the secret of remaining in bliss on the head. You in your condition can only remain in the bliss state if you understand at the most fundamental level that it is something special, something to be cherished, something to be shared.

ME: *And this is how your entities feel all of the time that they are in existence?*

SE3: Yes, and they are in existence for as long as I require them to be. Don't get the wrong impression here. I don't create entities and then destroy them or remove sentience from them. Like your Source Entity, I could remove them from existence at any time, but I don't. There is no need to, for in real terms I have just started the work that I wanted to do.

Source Entity Three's Environmental Dimensionality

ME: *O.K., I would like to ask a standard question that I plan to ask all of the Source Entities that is about the environment/s that you have created. What are they like?*

SE3: In variance to the multiple layer/dimension environments that the first two Source Entities created, I only created one. If you are observant, this is similar to one of the environments that Source Entity Two created. All of the entities that I have created exist and work within this environment. If I was to illustrate the dimensional mathematics to you, it would look like this: 12x1x12x3. That's 432 dimensions.

ME: *That looks like a similar representation to that given by the first two Source Entities. What I mean is that it is a multiple of twelve and three.*

SE3: Correct. I am told that you have already been educated in the mechanics of the rules for dimensional construct by your own Source Entity.

ME: *That's right. It is within the text of my first publication.*

SE3: Then I will not bore you with similar details. Suffice to say, there are rules that we have to follow for creating dimensional constructs or environments for existence. Those rules are based upon the way that the Origin is constructed—hence, the use of three base dimensions to start the construction of a single dimensional environment at the lowest level and the multiplication of those dimensions by twelve levels, not forgetting the frequencies that exist within the dimensions.

ME: *When my own Source Entity created us, he said that he had a lapse of concentration that resulted in some of the entities being created had a lower level of ability than others. These are used to look after the universe that it created and are allowed to incarnate into simpler physical vehicles for their own evolution. What happened when you created your entities? How did you create them?*

SE3: The process for creating a sentient entity is the same for all Source Entities. It is also the same as that used by the Origin to create us. The creating entity must identify and segregate that part of itself energetically that it wants to use as the medium for creating the entities concerned. Please note this. We cannot create something out of nothing—specifically if it is to have its own sentience. For if nothing exists, then there is nothing to work with. A void without energy of any kind remains a void. In this respect, we must give up part of our own energy, energy with sentience, to create that which requires its own sentience. These creations remain part of us, contained within us but separate from us.

The lack of concentration by your own Source Entity resulting in entities of lesser faculty was a result of its own lack of interest in the process once it had started it off. It simply became more interested in something else. The beauty of its error is that it ended up with a plethora of unexpected opportunities for evolution; opportunities that it hadn't planned for, hence its decision to keep what it ended up with. In my case I did not have such a lapse of attention and created what I wanted to create in the first place. In this instance what I created was pure and it was this level of purity that gave me the idea to restrict the universe they were to exist within to the higher frequencies of bliss, to ensure that everything remained pure. Pure of Heart therefore means that purity, or lack of error, is at the center of everything that I have created and will create.

Source Entity Three's Universe

At this point in the dialogue with Source Entity Three, I was aware that we had discussed very little of the nitty gritty of the subject that I like to be involved in, namely trying to understand the makeup of its universes and what the entities that exist within it were doing in order to achieve the goal of all entities created by the Origin and its Source Entities—individual evolution. I had not even merely scratched the surface of the first two Source Entities and had only ventured slightly further with my own Source Entity. I felt that I had gotten off to a slower start with this Source Entity than with the others. I was dissatisfied with my progress and was eager to move on. My own Source Entity had a few words of wisdom to help me on my way.

SE: Do not be impatient with your progress, for you are dealing with energies that are totally alien to you. As a result, you will find it hard to align yourself with some of the frequencies, especially when you have been stuck in the demands of physical life. I note that you have noticed that you are drawn to the physical more than normal lately?

ME: *Yes, I have even found out that one of my spiritual friends has been experiencing the same. It's like we are being lured, like something is fighting back at the increase in the Earth's frequency.*

SE: This is exactly what is happening. Those of lower frequency are indeed fighting back. As a result, you and others are feeling the weight of this pull you from every angle, in every relationship, and in every pastime. Thus you are finding it difficult to elevate yourself energetically and, hence, feel that you are being dragged down. Worry not, for it will pass, and you will get stronger as you come to recognize where the influences originate that cause the pull towards the lower frequencies. Concentrate on Source Entity Three, and you will be O.K. Remember that Source Entity Three is also a finer frequency than previously experienced. This will also cause you to feel a little discontented until you align your energies better.

ME: *Thank you for those words of encouragement.*

SE: It is a pleasure, for you are taking on quite a task.

I then changed my attention to Source Entity Three.

ME: *We have talked very little about your universal environment so far, other than to explain the basics. I would like to learn more about your creations and what they are doing in the environment you have created for them. I would like to split this into a number of areas, which I will discuss separately as I am aware that I have jumped in at the deep end with you. So, first, can you tell me more about the environment you created?*

SE3:   As I previously stated, my universe is limited to allow my smaller creations to experience nothing but the higher frequencies—what you call the bliss state. I can see though that you want to know more of the details behind it.

ME: *Yes, please. It would keep the dialogue similar to that already achieved with Source Entities One and Two.*

SE3:   Mmm. Do not preconceive what the dialogue will be, for that will lead the conversation into a direction that is adverse to what it needs to be. Remember, we are trying to give information about ourselves to humanity that it needs to know, not what you think it needs to know. Your desire to fulfil certain requirements of your own may divert you from the opportunity to access more important information.

ME: *O.K., I understand, but I would still like to touch on these two main areas. Whatever happens after, I will leave up to you.*

SE3: Good. Now I will explain my environment and my entities and what they do in order to evolve further.

As we have already discussed, my entities exist within those dimensions and frequencies relative to the bliss state. Having said this, I realize that any energetic state above your current frequency can be classified as bliss, but this is several orders of magnitude above the highest level that the human race could achieve. Indeed, what you experienced by tapping into my energies is but a fraction of a fraction of a fraction of what my entities experience.

Contrary to what you might think, my entities do have areas of what you call planets, spherical constructs, and areas of local density, where they are able to work on what they are experiencing. The environment I created for them is not as multi-layered as yours because the areas of local density exist within the normal high frequencies of the environment and do not form their own environment as a result of their lower level. Everything exists within the same environment; I have no separation between dimensions and frequencies.

ME: *I have just received an image of a purple-yellow colored planet in an area of space that is pure white light. Our planets exist in dark lightless space.*

SE3: That is a result of the higher frequency of the environment. Your own physicality is bound by low vibration which is signified by the darkness of the space in-between the areas of density. My environment is not bound by low frequency, so the areas in-between are in lightness.

ME: *So if your creations exist in such high frequencies, why do they need areas of local density to work out their evolutionary tasks?*

89

SE3: They don't as such. It's just that some of them like to associate themselves with an object of density. Don't get me wrong here. When I say density, I mean areas where there are energies that stick together out of creation not by what you would call "molecular attraction." These areas are created and, in most instances, can be given individuality.

Planets Created by Smaller Entities

ME: *Our planets have individuality!*

SE3: Your planets are collective individuals; they are the creations of the galaxies and are, therefore, facets of the galactic mind. These are not. They are either fully separate or are lacking individuality altogether.

ME: *So planets in this environment . . . can I continue to call them planets?*

SE3: Yes, it will suffice as an explanation although it is not entirely correct as I will explain later.

ME: *[Planets] are created by the entities that live in your bliss-based environment as a method of providing some level of focus on a certain evolution-based project. They are "similar energies" that are bound together to create an object of sufficient size to allow any number of entities to co-exist/work together on evolving. Indeed, the planet or energetic construct could, in fact, be the project itself.*

SE3: Not bad. But note this: the planet or planets are created by the entities but not larger entities, such as in your galaxies. Also, they are not generally spherical as they are in your physicality for they are not created by molecular attractivity. They can be and are any shape, frequency, dimension, or a mixture of all. They can be used as housing, workshops, or as something created for pure pleasure. Some of the entities even create entities to live on/in these constructs. They do this to see how smaller versions of themselves manage on their own.

ME: *This seems a bit like life on the Earth.*

SE3: Theoretically speaking, it does have a certain similarity, but in essence it is not because they are not dealing with the same levels of discontinuity of self—this being your projections into the lowest physicality you can find and almost separate from your totality as a result. They create new entities from the surrounding energy; they do not separate themselves to create new entities.

ME: *Hold on. I thought that all entities with sentience were created by separation of the larger entity to create the smaller. This is how the Origin created you and the other Source Entities. In fact, I distinctly remember being told this by Source Entity Two.*

SE3: This is correct. But note that you have used the word "sentience." The rule that you have stated is to do with the creation of sentient beings. The entities being created by my entities are more akin to what you would call astral entities. These are energy given form with individuality but without sentience.

ME: *So do the planetary entities also have entities to exist in or within them?*

SE3: They do, but they are similar in function to those you have on Earth to maintain it. You would call them nature spirits. In essence, they are not anything like the nature spirits your planet has, for they have limited function, ability, and longevity. They are created to perform a function and when that function is completed, they return to the core energy that they were created from. They are like tools in a box, so to speak, but with the box being full of "manipulatable" energy only, not specialized tools. The maintenance of the planetary construct is relative to its ability to withstand evolutionary pressure, so the nature spirits created are made in order to modify the planet to allow it to cope with/adapt to the demands of the creating entities using the planet.

An Area of Local Density

SE3: Now, let me tell you something about these planets. Your current expectation is to see a spherical shape for a planet or, indeed, a star. Although this is a common, natural shape in the physical and energetic environments created by your Source Entity, it is not a necessary requirement. Many of my creations have created areas of local density of any shape that you could know or think of. In fact, to use the word "shape" would only lead you astray in your process of understanding; you would "go off at a tangent," so to speak

ME: *So what does a planet or area of local density look like in your environment?*

SE3: It does not necessarily need to look like anything. Most of them just are what they are: areas of local density where there is more energy of a certain type and frequency than any other. A planet does not need to be a physical solid to be useful in evolution. Just take your largest planet, Jupiter. It mostly exists in a frequency that you are not aware of yet and houses many energetic entities. What you see in the physical is merely a shadow of its totality. So with this in mind, I will try to describe a typical planetary construct in my environment.

First, here's a correlation with your own area of local density, Earth. Your Earth is quite unique in your universe/multiverse environment, for it has both energetic entities and physical entities to maintain its function. Your nature spirits work on the higher frequency levels, and all kinds of your plants and animals work on maintaining the lower frequency levels. On planets in my environment, we have only the energetic entities because there is no need for maintenance at such low levels. Don't forget each of your animals has a maintenance-based function to perform on your Earth. So as one form becomes extinct, the function that it performs is lost and the resulting level of maintenance is diluted in this area. Because none of my creations have created a planet that is so low in frequency, there is no need for such lower frequency levels of maintenance; therefore, we have no animals. That is not to say that the creating entities do not have a desire to create smaller entities to fill the spaces available in their planetary creation, for they do so for their own pleasure.

A typical construct does not have or need physicality, and so it does not have one. You might want to use the construction of your own clouds as an example you can relate to for this is how they would be perceived if they could be seen by your physical eyes.

Within the construct, which would be similar in size to two of your suns, the entities create further constructs and discuss their relevance within the work they are doing to help their evolution. These constructs have a function and form that is relevant to the work they are created for.

ME: *So do they create things like houses, tools, and transportation just like us?*

SE3: No, they have no need for transportation systems or places of shelter. The constructs that they make are for helping other entities evolve.

ME: *Hang on a moment. There are other entities than those you created to exist in this environment?*

SE3: Yes, of course. They are created as part of the initial environment.

ME: *What? Now I am confused. Please help me out here as I am starting to lose the thread of the direction of our conversation.*

SE3: There is a general rule that all the Source Entities use when creating: an entity can create other entities for evolutionary purposes, but if that entity is to have sentience and individuality, it must come from the energy of the creating entity. On the other hand, if that entity is to have individuality but not sentience, then it can be created from the surrounding energy. An entity that is to have sentience but be part of a collective must also be part of the originating creator's energy. Therefore, only entities that are created by the giving up or sharing personal energy can have sentience and evolve. Some of the entities in my bliss-based environment have given up part or half of their energy, which, of course, links back to the Origin for the sole purpose of creating sentient beings that can both evolve in their own right and add to their creator's evolution. Please note that all of them are considered as equals, even though they are potentially of lesser energetic content—that is, volume not ability. They are also aware that they are created by others from their own personal energy and as such are bound by their energetic and evolutionary imprint.

An Evolutionary Imprint

ME: *What is an evolutionary imprint? That is a description I have never heard before.*

SE3: An evolutionary imprint is something that is unique to my entities. Each entity chooses a route to attain its optimum evolutionary opportunity. Call it a road map, if you like, with certain points that need to be achieved at certain points in their evolution. To get to these points, each entity needs to have achieved a certain level of experience, creativity, and responsibility. Each of these are recorded as being achieved, being experienced, being planned but not reached and in the imprint. If an entity creates an entity with the intention of giving it sentience, it then also gives it that which the creating entity has experienced and the rest of the points on the evolutionary imprint.

ME: *They get a head start in their existence above that of their creators.*

SE3: That is correct. But in doing so, the creating entity has the ability to evolve at twice the speed, as there are now two entities using the same imprint.

Replication, Division and Merging for Evolutionary Acceleration

ME: *So you are saying that the original entities that you created are also able to create sentient entities for the purposes of their own evolution?*

SE3: In a nutshell, yes. But do not think that this is unusual, for you also create sentient beings, do you not?

ME: *You mean we couple together to breed new human beings in order to replace ourselves and increase the population so that more souls can incarnate?*

SE3: Yes. And do you not evolve are a result of the interaction between yourselves as parents and the smaller beings you call children?

ME: *I suppose we do, yes, but we also accrue karma points as a result. It is a double edged sword with us humans re-creating ourselves the way we do. It's a slow process and relies on us, in general, being dedicated to those that we give physical life to for the rest of our physical lives. Some people abuse this privilege whereas others are model children, parents, and grandparents.*

SE3: I have just experienced what you are talking about through your memories. I will say that those that are created are created instantaneously and do not have to go through such long-winded processes. Those that are created with the evolutionary imprint are party to all knowledge and experience immediately upon creation.

ME: *So they are clones, direct copies of the creators?*

SE3: They are not direct copies, for they are not able to create from the division of themselves; therefore, they cannot create sentient beings. They can create non-sentient individual beings, but as I have previously explained, they are made of energy that is available within the surrounding areas.

ME: *O.K., so what do these copies do to evolve and help their creators evolve?*

SE3: They do what they feel is required to evolve. It is entirely possible for a creating entity to create many, many copies of itself in order to accelerate its evolution.

ME: *Up to how many can they create? There must be a limit so they avoid diluting themselves too much.*

SE3: Correct observation. There is an upper limit where they create before they lose their energetic majority. This is dependent upon the original energetic content of the creating entity, for not all entities are of equal content. This is mainly to do with the merging together of entities to create a bigger creating entity. I will describe this further in a moment. Suffice to say, an entity has a generally accepted upper limit of around one hundred copies of itself before it starts to lose its cohesion as a creating entity.

ME: *So what happens to an entity that exceeds this number?*

SE3: It becomes as one with their creations and loses the ability to re-create itself in this way. Also, by default, it then creates a collective. Some entities elect to do this as part of their evolution whereas others elect to merge themselves with another creating entity to create a new collective—in this instance, a single individual entity of greater power if you want to call it that.

ME: *So why would entities want to merge together whilst others want to diversify to the point of loss of creativity?*

SE3: Simply to evolve in a different way than the other entities they were created with.

ME: *So an entity may decide to either divide itself up to the point of dilution of own ability to experience evolution as a supposedly lesser entity but still be collectively connected to those entities that it created, or it can merge with others to create a bigger more powerful being of combined experience, knowledge, evolution, and evolutionary imprint.*

SE3: Yes.

ME: *Can the entity that has split itself into the level that it loses its creativity, entity-wise, reverse this process?*

SE3: Once the process has been initiated, it cannot be reversed, that is, not by the will of the original entity on its own. Remember: the creating entity has created a high number of "sentient" entities. It cannot of its own violation remove their individuality or sentience, for this would be akin to killing that entity. It can, however, merge with a willing entity to create an entity of greater "creator" energy and, therefore, reinstate its position— that position being relative to the number of entities that elect to merge with the original of a creating entity. They cannot merge themselves to create a bigger more powerful entity; this can only be done with the original creating entity and the desire of one or more "created" entities to return to their source.

Returning to the Creating Entity

ME: *Do they lose their individuality when they return to their creator? This is one of the things that we all ask in the physical world of our creator, Source Entity One. In our instance, we still retain individuality but are a fully functioning part of Source Entity One. We can even leave the Source at will if required/requested in order to provide additional evolutionary opportunities.*

SE3: Yes, but this is understood by the returning entity. They know that they came from nothing, as indeed we all do since we are all ultimately creations of the Origin. However, they are also aware that once they have been created, they can be re-created by the creating entity in totality at a later date after they decide to return to their creator.

ME: *So does this happen a lot? Do entities elect to return to their creator, complete in the knowledge that they will no longer have individuality?*

SE3: This happens on a regular basis and is a direct result of the type of evolutionary work done by that entity. In essence, they become specialized in evolving within certain types of experience. Once they have evolved as a result of the work they have done within the experiential environment, they may then elect to become part of the whole again. However, when the creating entity needs to evolve in an area that would be best supported by that part of itself that was of optimal evolution in the proposed experiential environment, it re-creates that entity even at the potential expense of it losing its creating functions. The object here is not the concern over the loss of individuality but taking every opportunity that presents itself to evolve and working with it. This is something that you humans could learn. In their eyes, evolutionary progression is the number one priority; they have no concept of personal loss of individuality. This is one of the facets of existence in the levels of frequency that they exist in.

ME: *So the entities that are created by the creating entities are, in effect, entities that are created as tools for maximizing evolutionary opportunities whenever they arise. They are facets of themselves that are experienced in evolving in certain conditions and are created specifically to maximize that opportunity. They are given sentience and individuality to allow them to function in a fully autonomous way, maximizing the evolutionary opportunity. This is why they have the evolutionary imprint. They function exactly as the original creating individual, and the only difference is that they are focused upon the task that they were created for. That is why the original entity evolves at the same time as the created entity. Although they are separate, they are one and the same. They are like, for example, twenty entities experiencing twenty different evolutionary opportunities all at the same time—thus allowing the creating entity the opportunity to evolve at twenty times the speed that it could on its own.*

SE3: Correct. This is a good analogy and is the reason why the created entities have no qualm about returning to their creator and losing their individuality as a result. It's also the reason why the creating entity has no issue with losing its creative ability and becoming one and the same with its creations, albeit temporarily, because it knows that at some point one of the entities it has created will need to return to it because it will have finished its job.

ME: *But hold on. You said that the created entities elected to return to their creators earlier. This tells me that they have some level of free will on electing to return, and when they complete their job, they may actually elect to not return to their creator.*

SE3: This is, in fact, a decision that they may elect to take. However, they must have a valid reason for not returning to their creator.

ME: *So what constitutes a reason not to return to the creating entity when the created entity has clearly finished its job, evolved, and in the process pushed the creating entity up the evolutionary ladder?*

SE3: As part of the finalization of the existence of the entity, it needs to review what it has done to evolve in the way it has. In that instance, if the entity sees that the level of evolution could be optimized further by taking the direction of experience into a different direction, one that is not too distant from that already experienced but different, it would be enough to warrant investigation. It may decide that it needs to investigate this route further and, therefore, extend its time in individuality in order to take advantage of this evolutionary opportunity. It does this of its own violation and does not need the permission of the creating entity. You see in this instance the created entity is doing its job correctly. It is pushing the evolution of itself and the creating entity by maximizing its existence. When eventually all of the avenues of opportunity are taken, the entity will then consider that it has maximized its reason for individual existence and will elect to return to its creator.

ME: *So how often does a creating entity reach the stage where it is in the state that it is equal with its creations, and how long could it stay in that condition?*

SE3: I would say that almost every one of the creating entities has been in this state at least three or four times. Indeed, some of them have been in this condition ten or twenty times. You have to understand that these entities have been in existence for almost as long as I have and, therefore, have had many opportunities to evolve. How long they have been in this condition varies from entity to entity and how many of their creations are close to finishing their work. I will check on the imprints of my entities. (Pause)

Some have experienced equality for as little as 25 minutes whereas many others have experienced this condition for many millennia; it just depends on the timing of the creation of their entities. A good average would be in excess of 300-400 of your years.

ME: *You just mentioned that almost all of the creating entities experienced this condition. This implies that there are those that haven't.*

SE3: You are right. There are a handful of entities that have not reached that level of dilution. This is not an issue for they have experienced the evolution that they expected to achieve in their evolution imprint.

ME: *You also stated earlier that some entities merged together to create a larger entity. What is the reasoning for this? I thought that they were pretty powerful in their normal state?*

SE3: Although the creating entities are powerful in their own right, they gain additional facilities as a result of their merging together. In variance to the re-merging together of created entities were the created entities that lose individuality when returning to the creating entity. When they merge together, they do not lose their individuality even though they are, for all intents and purposes, a single entity.

ME: *So what is the benefit of their merging then?*

SE3: Enhanced creativity which enhances their evolutionary opportunities. I see that this is not a good enough answer for you, so I will elaborate further. Creating entities that merge together in—I will use a word in your mind—coadunation, increase their capacity for creativity to a level that none of them could achieve on their own even in collaboration. In merged groups of three or four entities and above, they can create their own universes and act as a Source Entity might in terms of its level of creativity and resulting responsibility. This can only be achieved in numbers merging above two since three and above creates a critical mass that allows certain Source Entity energies to be available.

ME: *Do you have many creating entities merging?*

SE3: It is one of the most popular ways of enhancing evolution, especially when some of the creating entities elect to work within the universe/s that some of these merged entities create.

ME: *Do any of these entities remove themselves from this merged state? I can imagine that once an entity has experienced a level of creativity and responsibility consistent with the number of entities merged together that allows the integration of Source Entity energy, they would not want to return to a level that is, to my mind, fairly mediocre in comparison.*

SE3: You forget that these entities already exist in a fine frequency level, a bliss state, so they are not disenfranchised too much when they remove themselves from the merge. They have grown as a result of the merge and the energies involved and are "bigger" as a result. Suffice to say, I have only had two groups dissolve their merge to date and less than twenty individuals remove themselves from a merge greater than two. You may actually have a point here, but I . . . I will just scan them. (Pause) No, none of those who are still in a merged existence are only in that existence through fear of loss of ability, function, or power.

A Comparison with Source Entity One's Multiverse

ME: *One of the things I would like to ask is how similar is life, energetically and physically, in our multiverse compared to your own?*

SE3: You need to understand that there can be no comparison with your universe's environment—at least not in the sense that you would want a comparison to be made. As I've previously explained, the reason for this is due to the high frequency level of my universal environment. I can see that you are already about to ask another question, one where you think we may be able to make a comparison. Is this not correct?

ME: *Yes, I was thinking that we could compare the structure of your universe with that of Source Entity One's.*

SE3: First, your source Entity has created myriad different universes, which you call a multiverse. I chose not to go down this route as this was not what I wanted to do. As I have previously stated, I created a single universal environment of high frequency of an equally high dimensional status. Within this I have created one race of beings to populate it, each pre-programmed (as you are) with the need to evolve through experience. As my creations are all part of the same frequency base as their environment, they are subject to the limitations of that frequency. In my universe I also have one operational dimension; this dimension is singular in expression but high enough not to need the support of other dimensions to keep it in its position. If I were to compare its position with your dimensions, it would be in the 14-15th dimensional position. Bear in mind that you do not actually have a dimension of such a high status. In your multiverse, you have but twelve real levels within which all your other dimensions or dimensional phases exist.

ME: *My Source Entity told me that it had 12x12x12x3 dimensions. Are you saying that this is not true?*

SE3: It is true, but you have to consider that Source Entity One's dimensions are nested. It has created dimensions within dimensions, each of them padded out with a frequency base. My dimension is not nested and, therefore, allows an entity to access its volumetric opportunities in entirety.

ME: *Help me out here. Are you suggesting that the dimension in your universe is the same size as all of the dimensions in my Source Entities multiverse?*

103

SE3: Yes. It must be. We are both the same, so whatever we create, we create within ourselves. As a result we can make things as big or as small as we like, provided they are contained within our own boundaries.

ME: *I find that fascinating.*

SE3: You may, but it is one of the rules we, as Source Entities, have to follow.

ME: *Getting back to the comparison—if your entities are existing in a single dimension of high frequency, everything that they are in contact with must be the same because energetically speaking, they are based upon this. They must be in conflict with it at all times— like they must be stuck in the ground or a rock, so to speak.*

S3: You are thinking in terms of the physical environment that that part of you is currently experiencing.

ME: *I might be. I have to actually. This is the only tangible datum I have as a human being.*

SE3: Again, this is a physical consideration. Please understand—physics is the only known constant that can be used to describe that which is Origin, but know this: physics is not a study of the physical. It is a study of the energetic, and the energetic behaves relative to that dimension/frequency that it is part of. As a result, that which is of the same dimension or frequency is not necessarily in conflict. I will use your condition as a descriptor; it is not solid object against solid object. It is like a very rare gas mixing with a very rare gas. Of course, this is a crude example, and even the rare gas example is far too dense to be anywhere near correct, but it will suffice.

ME: *But aren't gases based upon differing frequency levels?*

SE3: No, they are based upon a different chemical composition, and a chemical composition is a physicality that is not available in my universe. Now consider that the difference in an entity and its environment is based upon energy—energy that is based upon a dimensional condition without actually needing to be part of a particular dimension—and you have the ability for that entity to have energy that is singular to its environment whilst being part of it because it exists within it. That means that the content of the universe is not opaque; it is always clear. An entity can pass through it, any part of it, at will without hindrance or resistance of any sort. I can see that you are having difficulty with this.

ME: *I am a bit.*

SE3: Well, think of it in these terms: the entity is one with the universe, and the universe is one with the entity. The only difference is that the universe has a single intelligence/sentience of its own. Parts of it also have intelligence and sentience. These smaller parts travel around the universe by associating that part of their intelligence where they want it. This causes the loci of their energetic signature—if you want to call it that—to be relocated to that part of the universe where they wanted to be present. Hence, this gives the impression that they have moved without hindrance.

ME: *Why did you use the word "loci"? It is usually attributed to a number of points a fixed distance from an originating point that creates a curve or that can be related to a specific point on a curve.*

SE3: That would be a good description of my entities. They have an origin point and other points where their intellect is in focus. When a particular point is in more focus than the others—that is, it has more sentience attributed to it—then it could be called the loci or locus of that entity. It is similar to that part of you that is typing this text now is the locus of that part of you that is projected into the physical of your multiverse to create you as a human being. Thus, they have a locus to indicate that that is the majority of them in their

105

universe. This is how they maintain their singularity within the universe and how they can become merged—by the joining together of points of their loci—or separated by removing points of their loci.

ME: *O.K., so I have established that you have created a singular universe and that it is of a high dimension and frequency. The universe has its own sentience, and it is populated with a single race of entities that have the ability to merge or split themselves up into smaller entities. The planets or areas of local density, if we can call them that, have no more density than a cloud in my planet's atmosphere. The entities evolve by being creative in their own right.*

SE3: That would be a reasonable summary.

Working Together—A Job for Life!

ME: *I can't help feeling that I am missing something though. It's like there is a piece of the jigsaw that is necessary before I can finish with my dialogue with you.*

SE3: You want to know what my entities do when they are attracted to work within the vicinity of local density you call planets.

ME: *Right!*

SE3: Then I will tell you as I can see that you want to get down to the coal face/nitty-gritty/basic levels of existence in my universe.

ME: *Correct.*

SE3: My entities do not need to have the trappings of life that you have in your universe and, therefore, do not use or create them. In your universe the entities that are incarnate are bound by the need to create objects of technology to help with everyday existence. Good examples are safe areas where you go to regenerate—you call them houses—and various means you use to

106

allow the physical body to travel from one part of the planet or universe to the other. Some of you even have devices that allow inter-dimensional transport. None of these are necessary in my universe.

As we have recently discussed and you have expressed eloquently, my entities can merge or separate to evolve in the way they choose. When they work together as a team, they do so as a team of merged entities, a team of separated entities, or a mixture of both. When they are working as a team, they sometimes find it advantageous to work within an environment where they are limited in their connectivity with the rest of the universe. To do this, they align themselves to the area of local density you call a planet. Now I have previously stated that the planets in my universe are not solid in nature; as a result, they do not have what you would call physicality. In fact, they are not part of a solar system or a galaxy which are clusters of areas of local density within your own universe, for they do not exist.

ME: *So the planets are singular and not part of a cluster in any way, shape, or form?*

SE3: No, but they are spread out fairly equally around my universe. Yes, I see that you have picked up an image of what I am describing. Think of a matrix in what you might call 3D. Then consider my universe as spherical that is filled with this matrix of areas of local density. You will then have a very crude illustration of how my universe is populated with planets.

Figure 1: The Matrix Sphere

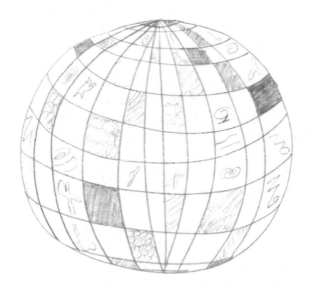

ME: *So how large are they?*
SE3: Some of them are as big as one of your galaxies whereas others are no bigger than your moon. They are all there for the use of my entities in their evolutionary exploits if they so wish to use them.
ME: *This is very interesting—a single universe with no galaxies but full of areas of local density or cloud-like planets with some of them as big as a galaxy in my own universe but, nevertheless, a planet. I can hardly think of the possibilities that present themselves in a planet the size of a galaxy. What do the entities do?*
SE3: I have explained some of the things they do from a high level already, but I can see that you still want something extra.
ME: *I do. I would like to understand what life is like being associated with these planets, even if it is a case that they just mess around with energy for hundreds of years.*
SE3: The planets are not solid, and so the entities that associate themselves with the planet work within them,

that is, in the area where the planet exists. The entities work with those that they are merged with or are split up as a group. Whilst operating within the confines of these planets, the entities' general objective is to use the available energy within the volume of the planet to create something of evolutionary benefit both to themselves and to those merged or separated but grouped entities at a later point in existence.

ME: *So what do they create? Considering that it is just a level of density that is lower than the surrounding universe, I can't imagine much.*

SE3: If they are to work within the planetary confines, then they are restricted to use only the energies that are available within this area. As previously stated, they create things that are of evolutionary importance. Some of these things may be constructs that, in turn, use the surrounding energies and turn them into something else of use that would not have been naturally available using the raw energies.

ME: *So you are talking about the creation of a new material by creating an energetic alloy of some sort?*

SE3: In short, yes, but these constructs may even create a finer energy set than that available in the universe.

ME: *Are you suggesting that they can create a better universe than the one where they exist but within the confines of the planet they are working with?*

SE3: Yes, this is one of the major reasons for my entities being in existence—to see if they can create something that is an improvement on where they exist—that being the universe and not the planetary environment that is the bliss state.

ME: *Is there not a chance that it would create a hole in your own universe, a hole that is filled with an environment of improved/increased/refined frequency?*

SE3: Yes, exciting isn't it? You see, what my entities are doing when they create an area of improvement is creating a new but localized universe. Within this universe they can do whatever they want, and they do! I will give you an example of an area of betterment that was created by one group of merged entities.

This group created a universe and populated it with entities they created themselves. These were then given the power of creativity themselves and, henceforth, created their own universe and populated it. This created a universe within a universe, which was a part of a planet in the total universe. Each of these universes had a dimension and frequency that was consistent with the total universe whilst being a microcosm of that universe. Within the first level of universe, the creating entities also created entities that were not given the power of creativity but were given purpose—that purpose being an automatic response to the needs of the creating entities.

ME: *What was that purpose? Was it similar to the roles that the nature spirits have in my universe, or was it something else?*

SE3:   If you are alluding to the need for your nature spirits to maintain the integrity of your earth and its surrounding area, then the answer is yes. The whole point of them being created was to help with the continued existence of the created universe and its contents. These universes or created constructs have a limited period of existence or usefulness if left unattended. As a result, those entities that are created for automatic purposes have but one role: to ensure that the creative intention is maintained.

Creative Intention

ME: *You've lost me. What do you mean by "creative intention"?*

SE3: You have this is your own universe; thought is part of your creative intention. The only difference is that when you use your creative intention and create something—whether an object or a situation—that which you have created remains in existence, unless of course it is transposed into another energy for some other reason. Within the universe that my entities have created, they need to create entities that maintain the intention that created the universe where they have been created to exist. In other words, they are the choir that continue the song that is started by the choir leader/s. Their sole purpose is to maintain the field of energy that keeps the universe inflated and maintains all that was created to exist within the universe, including themselves.

ME: *That must be quite a job, knowing that if you lose concentration and any part of the creative intention, you might wink out of existence.*

SE3: These entities do not know of that possibility, for they are not sentient. Their existence is infinite or until the creating entities decide to deconstruct the universe they have created, if in fact they do decide to deconstruct it at all.

ME: *So if these entities need to create entities to perpetuate their creative intention, what are they doing that means they can't maintain their own intent?*

SE3: They are creating elsewhere within the planet where they have aligned themselves. Therefore, they need to divorce themselves from the creative intention surrounding their creation of their universe before they can continue to create anew.

ME: *So these entities are the equivalent of pit props?*

SE3: In a word, yes.

ME: *Are there any other entities created for the maintenance of the "universe within a planet" creations?*

SE3: I can see that you are thinking of the equivalent of animals in your own universe.

ME: *Well, I was thinking of both physical and energetic, not just physical.*

SE3: Animals have a role to play in your own physicality, for they exist in order to maintain the ecosphere. The answer is no. The other entities created to help maintain other areas of creative thought are and cannot be considered as animals, for they are created purely for the use that they were created for. Your animals have another important role to play; they are your companions in the depths of low frequency physicality.

ME: *So in that case would you call them energetic machines because they seem to be doing the job of a machine?*

SE3: No, they are more than that as well. They are cognizant of the needs of the energies that they work with to maintain the intention that creates the universe they are working with, for intention is energy as well. There has to be a certain level of autonomy in their existence to allow them to work with the ebb and flow of intention energy.

ME: *What do you mean by ebb and flow? Does this energy increase and decrease?*

SE3: Of course. The energy of intention is made available by the creating entity each time the creating entity creates the intention to create something, no matter how small it is. Once the creating entity has delivered its intention for the universe it is working with/within, that energy has to be continued, especially if the intention is to create a permanent creation. This is what these entities are for— to continue the intention energy that is required to continue the creation. Now let's get back to the ebb and flow. The intention energy is only required whilst that creation is required to be present. When a creation is no longer required, the intention energy that created it is returned to the creating entity; therefore, the energy of the maintaining entity is reduced as is the workload for continuing the existence of that creation.

ME: *Hold on here. Are you suggesting that the maintaining entity has to sustain, hold in the present, the thought supporting the intention?*

SE3: Yes, that is its workload. On top of that, one of the main pieces of work it has to do is to maintain the thought that created the intention energy that created itself. It, therefore, has incentive to continue its work.

ME: *But at some time the creating entity will need to remove the intention energy that is maintaining its own existence.*

SE3: Yes, but that only happens when the group of entities that have created the universe decide to close it down and when all the evolutionary opportunities apportioned to that universe have been experienced by those entities destined to experience them. In this instance, the creating entities assume control of their own intentions and remove them from the wider universal matrix--thus, removing the universe. Suffice to say, a decent size universe has a long time before it reaches this point in its existence. Sometimes new entities who were not on the original list may request the opportunity to experience that environment, thereby extending its existence beyond that planned.

ME: *What would one of these intention energy maintenance entities look like?*

SE3: You are typically human and need to see everything.

ME: *Yes, I do.*

SE3: I was advised of this by your Source Entity.

ME: *I am sorry, but it helps with my understanding and allows me to explain to others who want to understand in a way that they will comprehend.*

SE3: I will describe one of them for you then. If you were to see them with your energetic eyes and then overlay that image onto your cerebral cortex, they would appear as a ball that is full of stars of differing colors. Each of the stars represents a level of energy that is related to a particular intention. The color of the star represents the level of attention and intention the maintaining entity needs to sustain to keep it manifest.

ME: *I can just see an image in my mind's eye. The image I see is a ball full of stars, but the entity has only white stars with a couple that are blue.*

Figure 2: The Ball Filled with Stars

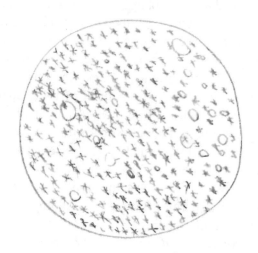

SE3: Yes, good. That is an example of an entity that has an even level of attention required but with two intentions that are not so important.

ME: *Why would an intention be of lesser importance?*

SE3: Because the opportunities it offers have all been used up; therefore, the intention is close to being returned to the creating entity. The color is representative of the number of entities taking advantage of the intention for evolutionary purposes. The blue color, therefore, indicates that only a few entities are using the creation created by this intention.

ME: *O.K., I would like to give the readers an idea of what the universal environment would look like if it were to be seen with physical eyes.*

SE3: You would need to use the process that I described above because you would not be able to perceive it otherwise. Consider that you are in the center of what you call the northern lights, the aurora borealis. The magnetic properties of the planet where you exist manipulates the universal (cosmic) energy in a way that provides a reasonable example of what it may look like on one of its levels.

ME: *It's full of different colors.*

SE3: Yes, but that's not what I am looking to describe. It's the energies and how they are being manipulated by the magnetic flux is what I am referring to. In this instance, the magnetic flux can be used to describe an entity, and the colors in the atmosphere represent how that energy is responding to the manipulation. Of course, the colors are just one manifestation of what is happening to the energies under the influence of the magnetosphere, one that you can perceive, but it gives you an idea as there are many levels of magnetic flux in the magnetosphere. The effect it has on the universal energies is not within your range of perception. Suffice to say the universal environment that my entities manipulate reacts in a way that can be described in this method. The planetary environments would, therefore, be a subset of energies that are held in place by a single energy. This allows my entities the opportunity to use other energies, together with their intention, to manipulate them at will and thus create their own universes and entities.

115

As I have stated before, physicality is not available in my environment. Entities exist in the higher level of frequencies that are associated with bliss, so there is no datum within you that I can use to allow a more in-depth description of me and my creations.

I will leave you now so that you can contemplate that that you have been given.

In Closing: A Word from the Origin

And with that Source Entity Three was gone. There was no more contact. I tried to raise my energies and awareness to encompass my higher aspect, going well beyond the levels where I initially made contact with our own Source Entity and up at the periphery of energy that I knew was the Origin. This was a place that I expected to be able to log back into the entity that I was just in communication with, but all I got was the image of all the Source Entities, all bunched up together forming that part of the Origin that it had dedicated to being separate but within itself to assist in its quest for further self-awareness, understanding, and evolution.

The Source Entities below me appeared as a group of dark colored opaque balls. Each ball houses the intelligence that is a Source Entity and its creations, universal and multiversal environments together with the entities that occupy them. I experienced a sense of awe that I was once more in this area of the Origin, outside the boundaries of my Source Entity and in the in-between area—that area that is beyond the Source Entities and before the outer layers of the Origin, that area that is and can only be the Origin itself. I sought contact with the Origin with a view to gaining further insight.

ME: *It has been some time since we spoke, for I have been concentrating on communicating with my own Source Entity and Source Entities Two and Three.*

O: Yes, and you still have the others to communicate with as well. This is not an easy job you have chosen here because your frequency is in variance to all but your own Source Entity and, of course, Me.

ME: *I feel that once I have established a link with the Source Entity I am communicating with, I can communicate with it. I do have to say that I end up being far more fatigued communicating with the other Source Entities than I do when I communicate with my own creator. I also feel that, so far, the depth of information that I am receiving is not what I expected.*

O: You expected more detail?

ME: *In a word, yes.*

O: If you would check with the level of detail you have gained from your own Source Entity and compare it with what you have gained from your communication with the other two Source Entities, you would notice that it is of a similar depth. The only difference is that in the first book you have delved a little deeper into the human aspect of Source Entity One's environment.

I took the time to examine mentally the information about the first book that was in my mind and found that the Origin was correct. The detail and depth were similar. There was still something missing though. The Origin responded to me before I had the chance to ask the question.

O: Remember, it would be an impossible task in your current form to assimilate all the information that is in just one universe that your Source Entity created, let alone what is in any of the other universes, dimensions, and frequencies. The information that you have been given is a microcosm of the greater reality—not that it is

117

unimportant. Any level of information that brings the truth to the lower frequencies is important, and each of the entities that have taken on this noble work is only capable of glimpsing and taking on-board a small part of the picture, a single piece in an extremely large jigsaw puzzle.

Something else to consider is that you are not alone in this work, for many have chosen to take on an aspect of the delivery of the truth to mankind. No one of you could do it on your own, nor would it be desirable for you to do it on your own because humankind is not able to assimilate such knowledge in the volumes that would be necessary to support such information. It has to be and is being done at the speed and volume that is optimal for the absorption of such knowledge in the projected consciousness of those who are interested, becoming aware, and exposed to those who are interested and becoming aware.

Therefore, the work you are doing is both at the correct level, to plan, and in the correct event period. The only other advice I would give you is to not get despondent when you feel communication is both difficult and slow when communicating with the other Source Entities because you are working with energies that are not normally experienced by entities in Source Entity One's environment. I would also ask you to enter your higher aspect more, for that will allow your energies to become more aligned with my energies than they are now. This will help in making your communication with the remaining Source Entities less tiring because you will be using a more universal energy medium than the one that is specific to the Source Entity that created you. Thus, you will not need to rely as much on the hidden translatory function that your Source Entity is providing.

ME: *Thank you. I will endeavour to do my best in this instance.*

O: Just one more word of advice about when you reach the level of your higher aspect. As you work with this level of your "self" more and more, you will feel disassociated with the physical plane of your existence. You must be careful of this as it will affect your physical judgement and ability to discriminate correctly when interacting with those of the physical plane who work around and with you.

Go now and work with this information and commence communication with Source Entity Four.

Chapter 4

Source Entity Four

Source Entities One, Two and Three had proven to be an ice-breaker for me as I was a little bit concerned that I would not be able to hold the energy long enough to be able to communicate for any length of time. That is not to say that I found the communication with Source Entity Three easy. Some of the time I felt very fatigued, especially when I was in a position of receiving information that I clearly understood from a perceptual basis but simply did not have the language to describe it, such as the difference in the environments that I have been exposed to. I was thinking about this and what wonders Source Entity Four (SE4) would expose me to when Source Entity One, the entity responsible for creating everything I/we know, decided that it was time that I got off the proverbial fence and started to learn the communication process that would result in my ability to link directly with Source Entity Four.

SE: It is time to be elevated to the next level of communication. The Origin has advised me that you must start immediately since the energies that surround you and those you have been exposed to whilst communicating with Source Entity Three will provide a useful springboard for your alignment to the energies that are fundamental to the communication with the fourth Source Entity.

ME: *What do you mean? The environments of Source Entities Three and Four are of similar frequency?*

SE: No, the frequencies used in the creation of the environments associated with Source Entity Four are even higher than that of Source Entity Three. The problem here is that the gap in the frequencies from those that you are used to and aligned to in my multiverse is too big to make the communication possible without first being elevated for a period of time. In essence, you need to be normalized. The process of normalization would normally take a few weeks to achieve if we were starting from scratch, but as you already have a residual level of higher and differing frequency, we can make the jump to the level and type of frequency required in one go. This is something that will be commonplace with you as you start to work with the other Source Entities, for the more you are in contact with them, the easier you will find the communication. Indeed, the adaptation to such frequencies will also enable you to understand what you are experiencing better and give you the language to use in its description for your texts.

ME: *From my perspective it would seem that the frequencies in your multiverse are lower than the other Source Entities.*

SE: That is not the case; it is just that they are different. There is one point to note though—only a few of us have decided to create environments that go down to the lower frequencies and dimensions of the Origin. As a result, you will not experience many things that you would consider to be similar to your own current condition, for your current condition is in the lowest of the physical frequencies.

Let us delay no longer, for during this short conversation I have been elevating and modifying the characteristics of your higher frequency physicality so that you can make contact with Source Entity Four. You may start whenever you are ready.

The dialogue with my own Source Entity stopped, and I was on my own again. The dialogues with my own Source Entity were now so common it was like talking to a friend sitting next to me; as a result, the room then felt empty. I concentrated on the task at hand—connecting with the energies that would link me to the entity that I would spend the next three months communicating with. I had no idea what the energies would feel like, just that I had been aligned to them in some way by my own Source Entity. Just as I finished typing the last sentence, I felt my body start to tingle and a great weight suddenly came into my head.

Initial Contact

ME: *Is that Source Entity Four contacting me?*

SE4: It is, I have been waiting for you and you appear to be stalling! So I decided to initiate the contact myself rather than wait for you.

ME: *This I didn't expect, a Source Entity contacting me. It was usually the other way round.*

SE4: We have many things to discuss and not much time to do it in. What do you want to discuss first?

ME: *I have a loose format* (I was starting to realize that the rigidity of my initial format stemmed the flow of information). *I would like to understand how and when you became conscious, what made you decide on the type of environment you created, and what entities you created to populate that space. Also, I would also like you to describe both the environment and the entities.*

SE4: You do not want much; let me see how I can help without making it too difficult for you. I will start with the wakening, for your own Source Entity has advised me of your format, what you like to discuss, and in what order. But know this, I will diversify when I feel that the information I am giving you is too similar to that given to you by the other Source Entities for there is a certain level of crossover resulting from the very nature of what we are, facets of the Origin.

ME: *O.K., I get it. There are similarities between the environments created by the other Source Entities— similarities that, if included in my texts too often would detract from the message I am trying to bring to the public of Earth.*

SE4: Correct. I will begin. I was one of the first to become aware of who and what I was. That is not to say that that makes me any better than the others. It is just that I had a spontaneous understanding and not a gradual awakening. It was like you being asleep one moment and then awake the next. Although I did not have a full set of memories of my existence like you do about your current existence, I was in the knowledge of the fact that I was created by the Origin and had a job to do. That job, I also knew, was the same as the others that I found around me.

ME: *What did the others look like from your perspective?*

SE4: They were just as you see them when you position your perception and intelligence outside of your Source Entity; we were like a bunch of black shiny balls all bunched up together. One or two of them would periodically move out of the bunch and change their shape and form or even create things in front or around them.

ME: *I just received an image of one of the Source Entities creating a pinky purple cloud in front of them.*

SE4: Yes, that was the Source Entity you will refer to as Source Entity Six (SE6). It is quite a character and is always up to what you might call "mischief."

ME: *Mischief? How can a Source Entity be up to mischief? I thought you were all very responsible beings.*

SE4: Of course, we are, but we do have personality as well. You have experienced this in some ways already. It's just that you have ignored it. As I started to describe my awakening, I will continue in this vein.

It took me a bit of time (I use this phrase for your help not mine, by the way) to recognize that I had, in fact, just jumped into existence fully aware. My memory of events started from a single point that was not too far away from my realization of lack of long term memory. I shelved that thought for a number of times as I was becoming more interested in what was going on around me as the other Source Entities were becoming aware and were experimenting with energy and form. Their experimentation was a distraction to me in my self-analysis; as a result, I forgot about my questioning of self. I had started to do what they were doing as it seemed the right thing to do at that time.

ME: *So what did you do? I have already received some information of what you all did in the first millennia of your existence, but I like to know what each individual Source Entity did directly from itself.*

SE4: As I said, at first I was questioning my "self," but my attention was drawn to what the other Source Entities were doing. They were just experiencing themselves in every way possible—from creating what you would call "shapes" out of their energy and external form to creating duplicates of themselves on every possible dimensional and frequential level. I copied them for a while—repeating everything that each of them did to and with themselves. This did not last long though as I was more interested in looking into what I wasn't and exploring that.

ME: *What do you mean—what you weren't?*

SE4: Each of us has areas that are not part of us. They are what you would call "voids." I found the fact that there were voids in me most interesting.

125

ME: *How can you have voids? Does my Source Entity have voids?*

This was a bit bizarre to me and is not something that I had come across in any of my previous communications with the Source Entities I had been in contact with or the Origin.

SE4: All Source Entities have voids. One of the things I was, therefore, very interested in was the reason why we have these voids. This was my major distraction before I returned to the question of "self" although you could argue that they are both part of the same thing.

ME: *So where were these voids? I can imagine that they would be areas where you have a local lack of density, energetically speaking.*

SE4: This is not the case. The location of a void could be directly central to an area of what you might call dense energy; it can also be located within an area of sparsely populated energy as well as on the interface of dense and fine energy. I found out that this is a function of us.

ME: *Please explain what you mean by "function of us." How can the population of energy be a function of you?*

SE4: I will give you the example of function and form.

As an entity projected into an extremely densely populated area energetically, you should be aware of the fact that some parts of you are denser than others and all these parts have a function. For example, your liver has the function to help clean the blood in the physical and to regulate the flow of energy in the energetic. The blood itself is not so dense and is, therefore, a fluid, with the job to carry oxygen and nutrients to the rest of the body and the larger organs. Its job energetically is to create a framework of the universal energies that are used in your energetic bodies that your healers call astral levels 5, 6 &7, which act as an energy cage keeping the correct energies in and around the body and repelling those that are not necessary to the continued function of the physical vehicle. Within your physical body you have voids, areas in-between organs, bone, muscle, and veins (arteries). These voids allow for the expansion and contraction of these organs during various stages of function. Voids are also present as a result of the "incompatibility in form" factor of the organs, bone, etc.—the form factor being correct for the function they have but not for their efficient fitting together in the jigsaw puzzle that is the physical human body. This is the same for us.

ME: *Wait a minute. Are you insinuating that Source Entities have organs, areas of energy that have specializations, jobs to do? I thought that you were purely energetic.*

SE4: We are purely energetic, but we do have areas of energy that have specific jobs to do. This is what I found out when I was making my investigations into self. One thing that you need to understand though is that these specialized areas of energy—and they are all over us— are part of our function that enables us to be who we are, separate whilst still being part of the Origin. The voids are just areas where there is no need for function and, therefore, no need for energy—that is, energy of any sort. The voids are an interesting factor though. I am finding out that some of the entities I created use them to traverse from one part of me to another. With there being no energy, there is, therefore, no resistance to movement. We can talk about this in greater detail later because I want to give you more detail on how my colleagues and I are made up.

ME: *O.K., carry on. I find this a most interesting development.*

SE4: As I said before, each of us has areas that have energies that have function. These functions are for the use and the maintenance of "self" with a view toward perpetuation. It would be best if I list these functions first and then explain their jobs in a little more detail later. They are as follows:

- Structure
- Form
- Volume
- Detail
- Compartmentalization
- Singularity
- Diversification
- Multiplicity
- Self
- Remembrance
- Being

Structure is the first function of a Source Entity. It is independent and interconnected with form and volume, irrespective of energy or its type. It is what we are, and it maintains our level of inflation, so to speak. Every entity has structure of some sort, no matter how diverse it is.

Form is what we choose to be to maximize the number of environments we create. It is interconnected with structure and volume. Form does not necessarily relate to shape since it is a function of division and the energies required to maintain that division. It can also be connected with compartmentalization when creating independent unconnected environments.

Volume is how we choose to inflate ourselves in order to accommodate the environments and the entities we create. It is interconnected with structure and form. As with form, volume also has a link with compartmentalization as I can change my volume in certain areas of myself to allow the creation of an environment to take account of all energy of a specific type if I so wish. This is specifically useful if I want to have an experiment with an environment that is filled with a single energy type. Depending upon what maintenance function is being performed, volume also increases or decreases.

Detail is what is being investigated by every one of us, including the Origin. It is the detail of "self" that gives us our individuality, our being, our personality if you like. Although every one of us has been created in equality, it is the detail that tells us apart.

Compartmentalization is what we do when we create an environment. It is a function that allows our normal functionality to operate without the need to maintain that environment that has been compartmentalized. We can place the environment on automatic, so to speak, or entrust the environment's maintenance to a group of entities created for such a function. Your own Source Entity has done this for your environment. From a creativity point of view, it is a particularly useful function as it means that neither the environment created nor I contaminate each other.

Singularity is a function of being and detail. It is what keeps us autonomous from the Origin. Being a singularity means that we are responsible for ourselves and the maintenance of our creations. We are given singularity by the Origin. It is a most special gift.

Diversification is a function of our ability to experiment with the different ways of evolving. When new ways are discovered, it is using these ways in parallel to accelerate our total evolution and ability to give such data to the Origin.

Multiplicity is a higher function of singularity and diversification. It is the ability to perform many, many things all at the same time. In your language it is my ability to be in contact with all of my self, my creations, and my environments simultaneously without loss of concentration. This is the omnipresence that your priests talk about. I do this because all my energies and creations are connected.

Self is that function of me that "is." It is a result of the correct and harmonious operation of detail and being. Self is what we all investigate at the start of our existence.

Remembrance is energy with a most important function. It is the way we continue to know who and what we are and what we have achieved. It is fundamental to the continued efficiency of the diversification function.

Being is a result of the combined functions of detail, self, and singularity. It is a higher function of self whilst being separate and independent whilst also being interdependent. It is what makes us Gods in the shadow of a greater God, the Origin.

ME: *These don't describe energies; they are all functions. In fact, thinking about it, they describe "conditions."*

SE4: All functions need energy to perform their tasks, so the basic component of any function is the energy that surrounds it. It's what makes it happen. Moreover, a function "is" a condition. In the examples I have just given you, I have very briefly described functions or conditions of my/our existence. You must take into account the fact that energy is the basis for everything that is in existence, from the smallest inert object to the largest entity, such as the Origin. Without it, there is nothing. That is, "no thing" that can be in existence, for there would only be void. A void does not contain energy; humanity does not understand this concept yet.

ME: *They seem to rely on each other for their own existence though.*

SE4: Of course, they do. This is the beauty of existence. It is dependent upon the harmonization of many factors or functions working together to create the whole—the whole entity that is me in this case. You have the same thing if you consider again your own physical/energetic body as an example. All of the components that make up the human physical and energetic bodies have a "collective" of organs that have specific functions to perform; each of them has interdependency with the other even if you don't recognize it yet. Some of them have a level of redundancy, and some can even be removed without too many detrimental effects on the whole. You can survive living with one lung, one kidney, one eye, or no appendix, for instance. You can even lose a chakra or two, provided you are not exposed to the conditions where you need ALL of your organs, physical and energetic. You can still exist, albeit in a state of reduced performance. The problem you have with this reduced state of performance is that you do not know what functions are missing that result in the reduced state of performance because you have not used them for such a long time. Your physical organs, therefore, have a set of higher functions that, in some instances, requires what you classify as redundancy or duplication. For example, did you know that your appendix has a higher function that is associated with the accumulation and distribution of what your spiritual healers have been calling "core star" energy?

ME: *No, I had no idea.*

SE4: Well it does, and its dysfunction is due to consumption of the wrong food.

ME: *How do you know this level of detail about the human body?*

SE4: All Source Entities share the knowledge they gain with the Origin and because we are the first creations of the Origin, we gain that which is given to the Origin from our counterparts.

ME: *So what one learns, you all learn.*

SE4: Yes, this is part of the requirement for existence at my level although to a lesser extent, all entities have the ability to learn from the experiences of other entities. The human part of the multiversal records in your own environment, the Akashic records, are an example of this, but it is more of a manual approach whereas mine is automatic.

ME: *Thank you. So let's return to functions and structure. The names you have used are not what I would use to describe the functions of the energies that keep you in existence as a Source Entity. I find it difficult to relate to the nomenclature versus the functions.*

SE4: The words I use are what are available in your vocabulary. In a lot of cases this is woefully inadequate. Hence, the words that I have used to describe my functional energies may not be optimal. Nevertheless, they will suffice.

ME: *So the voids in the energies, would they also have a function even though they are "void" of any energy?*

SE4: Their position is useful. The energy has to flow around such voids, and flow creates function. As I have stated before in one of my previous descriptions, the voids allow for the expansion and contraction of those parts of me that have work to do in the evolutionary sense. By this I mean that the environments that I create sometimes need to be bigger or smaller, depending on the number of entities working in them or the type of work they are doing.

ME: *Tell me more about the flow of energy and its importance in function.*

SE4: Those parts of me that provide my structure need to have energy flow to allow the function to operate. You see, energy is not and cannot be inert, static, or stationary. It needs purpose. Flow is, therefore, a product of purpose in energy. But let me tell you this: flow is not what you think it is. You think of flow as that which water does when it is moving in a certain direction or around an obstacle. Indeed, flow is and can be described as direction, but in this instance direction is best described as purpose.

ME: *So when you said that the energy has to flow around the voids in your structure, you meant that it has purpose. So what would that purpose be?*

SE4: Where energy has flow around the voids, its purpose is to maintain the boundaries between the void and the environment. Flow is also used to create a framework for an environmental construct and its habitation. It can be the barriers between environments, and it can allow travel between environments should you wish to do so.

Environments

ME: *I would like to move on to the construction and inhabitants of your creations if I may.*

SE4: Please do so.

ME: *How is your multiverse/universe constructed? In my dialogues with the other Source Entities, I have been advised on the level of dimensions and frequencies, and I learned that they are based on the number twelve, my own Source Entity having 12x12x12x3 dimensions.*

24 Dimensions and 2,322 Frequencies

SE4: I have a slightly simpler philosophy when it comes to such things, for I believe that too much complexity is detrimental to the task of evolution. In my instance, I have 24 dimensions and frequencies. That is 12x2x0x3 in your language.

ME: Now you have confused me. I would have thought that the method used to describe 24 dimensions would have been simply 12x2 not 12x2x0x3.

SE4: There is a universal constant that it is necessary to use in the construction of a dimension, and this is based upon the way that the Origin is formed. That means there needs to be a basis for the first true dimensional platform, which, in this instance, is three. It is also based upon the lowest dimensional condition. It is not frequency-based.

This is something that I see you are getting confused with, for you are mixing frequency and dimensional descriptors together in your mind.

ME: I thought I had got this straightened out during my dialogues with my own Source Entity.

SE4: Clearly not. Your Source Entity has stated that it has 12x12x12x3 dimensions, equating 5,184 dimensional environments, but there are still only 12 dimensions as described to you in your first book. Let me make it a bit easier for you. When you multiply the figures we have just discussed, you end up with a number of separate environments. Each of them has its own frequencies and frequency range. These are dimensional environments, not true dimensions, per se. In one of your previous communications with your Source Entity, you discuss the concept[1] that there are actually ten dimensions—the

---

[1] "I now understand that this is an incorrect statement (see Beyond the

first three equating to one true dimension with the remaining nine being a dimension in their own right because they all need the first three to be in place first before they can be in existence themselves because the first three are the basis for dimensional existence.

ME: *So if I use the description given to me during a previous dialogue, you have twelve dimensions within two environments.*

SE4: Not quite, for the way that I have constructed the compartmentalization of my environments is not based upon the need for nested or separated areas of existence. For instance, Source Entity Two has four environments with the dimensions divided into these four areas while I have simply used the whole of me to create 24 dimensions. Of course, if you use mathematics to explain the number of dimensions, you would get 72. In actual fact, the last number (three) as we have already discussed is really equal to one.

ME: *So you have 24 dimensions to play with, so to speak.*

SE4: Correct. Each of these dimensions is inflated with 2,322 frequency levels.

ME: *That's a strange number. Why 2,322?*

SE4: That is the number of frequencies used to create a useable environment without overlap. In your own environment your frequencies have peaks and troughs

Source, Book 2). The structure of SE1's environment is 12 full dimensions each constructed of 3 sub dimensional components, each of which is inflated by 12 frequency bands. Except those which created the foundations (our own universe), where the three sub dimensional components equal 1 sub dimensional composite component and therefore 1 full dimension, which is in turn inflated by 12 frequencies to create the first universal environment (our universe)". I have since recognised that the Source Entities let me be in some error due to the fact that, at a particular point in time, it would be too hard for me to understand the actual correct detail, and that what I understood was close enough to the truth to allow the thought process henceforth projected to mankind's memory to be of some significant use, in variance to receiving no information. GSN 14/04/2012 (During final editing) where it is possible to move into one frequency from another in areas where the peak of one frequency is in direct proximity with the trough of another. This is not possible in my environment since a true and substantial change in frequency by the individual entity is required for translation to occur. This is only possible through a significant change in evolutionary condition.

ME: So how many entities have you created to fill these 24 dimensional environments?

SE4: Fourteen thousand million, plus or minus a few hundred thousand.

ME: I thought that you would be able to pin that down to the last entity. Why the plus or minus?

Eternal and Non-eternal Entities

SE4: Whereas you have eternal existence, some of mine do not. This was a result of the creation process that I used. Creativity is not always perfect, a condition that your Source Entity is fully knows. As a result, some of them do not exist long and have to be re-created. In doing so, I create more than I previously created. I do this in order to compensate for those who are imperfect. This circle of creation has not yet been completed; eventually they will all be eternal, but that is a task that will be achieved later in my existence.

ME: So you created about fourteen thousand million entities with some of them not being eternal. How do you resurrect those that are not eternal when they expire, or do you just replace them with another entity?

SE4: I don't just replace them for I owe them continued existence due to my creation process, so in this instance, I work on the energies that they are made of and re-create them with the energies they should have. I can see that you are confused by my use of your language, so I will explain again. When I re-create these entities, I copy the essence of what they are both energetically and in experience—that is, those experiences and the resultant evolution content leave an impression on the energy that is the entity. In order for me to resurrect them completely, I need to re-create the energy that resulted in eternal beings and imprint the impression that their older energy had—the evolution content and the energetic personality, if you like, into the new energy that I have created in its entirety. This ensures their continued existence.

ME: *Do they know that they are substandard compared to the rest?*

SE4: No. In this instance I have withdrawn the memory of longevity from each of my creations until all of them exist in equality. Once I have finished this work, I will allow the knowledge that they are eternal to permeate into their energy field. Right now they don't recognize or, in fact, understand that they are or are not eternal. They just are, and the work that they are doing is interesting as a result.

ME: *How can an entity not know that they are not eternal when they clearly are? I am talking about the ones that are actually eternal here.*

SE4: I am surprised at you, for is not mankind largely unaware of its immortality?

ME: *You're right. At least currently in the physical we are unaware that we are eternal—unaware that the majority of us is energetic and only a small part of us is projected into these low frequencies where we exist in a very solid vehicle, the physical human body, to allow us to experience existence in the material part of this universe. But as both/either bystanders and participants in the death process, we experience the demise of the physical body on a regular basis while remaining totally ignorant of the fact that life in the physical is transitory. Your entities must experience this as well to some extent.*

SE4: They don't as they do not currently feel the need to experience existence at such low frequencies yet although the do experience physicality.

ME: *But they must know that they are eternal due to the long time that they have been in existence and the number of memories that they have of their experiences. They must remember these?*

SE4: As I said before, I remove the memory of longevity from all of my entities so that they do not know that they are eternal. I do this by only allowing them to keep the most recent memories and some other key memories, but I ensure that these key memories have the event location markers removed from them so that the entity cannot place the order or note the event where that knowledge was gained as the result of experience.

ME: *So where does that knowledge go to if it is removed from them on what I assume is on a regular basis?*

SE4: I keep it within myself with a view to passing it back to them all when they are all eternal.

ME: *That's an awful lot if information you must be keeping.*

SE4: Along with the other Source Entities, I have an area of energy within myself that is just for the retention of experience that is not only my own experiences but all of the experience gained by any of my creations. This is the same energy that passes on experience to the Origin. All I do is provide a level of compartmentalization to occur so that the experiences of each individual entity are assigned to the entity that experienced the experience. It is quite a simple routine and one that is automatically achieved once set-up. You have something similar in your multiversal environment; you call it the Akashic records. The difference between the two records is that in my set of records, the entity will only be able to access them all once I have given all of my entities eternal existence. On top of that, they will only be able to access their own records. They will not be able to access the records of any other entities within any of my environments.

ME: *I have just seen an image in my mind's eye that suggests that you have compartmentalized your entities into different sections within your twenty four dimensions. Can you explain what I am seeing here?*

SE4: Yes, of course, but I can see that you have an expectation I have separated those entities that are eternal and put them into one environment and those that are not eternal into another.

ME: *That thought had crossed my mind, but I can see that this is not the case from the way that you are leading this conversation.*

SE4: You would be right to think in that way. No, I have not separated them in that way and the reason why I haven't is actually quite simple. The reason is that I am gradually changing the energies of those entities that are not eternal to being eternal. If I had them compartmentalized into eternal and non-eternal environments, then I would have to move the entities that I have made eternal from the non-eternal environment into the eternal environment. This would upset the balance of the population of entities within each of my environments, which ultimately would result in the one that was full of non-eternal entities being empty. No, I have not separated them out for this very reason.

ME: *O.K., I would like to ask some questions.*

- *What are your environments like?*
- *Do they have physical aspects, such as planets etc.*
- *What are your entities like, how are they made up, and how would they appear to us?*
- *What are your entities doing?*
- *What are your entities creating? Do they need to create to evolve? [SE4: creativity is an essential*

and universal requirement for evolution]
- *How are they evolving?*
- *How are they organized/civilized?*

SE4: You have a lot of questions. It would be best to work on them one by one, as there may be many questions that come out of each. I think you would call them nested questions?

ME: *I believe that is correct.*

Constants Involved in Creation

SE4: One thing you need to note here is that there are a number of constants that are involved in the creation of an environment. These constants are what we are given by the Origin to work with and as a result you may find that some of the descriptions I give you may sound similar to those you have already received.

ME: *Actually, that is something that I am a bit concerned about. Will the readers of this text not think that this is all made up, that I am using my imagination and that as a result of the magnitude of this task, I am running out of ideas?*

SE4: They can think what they like. The truth of the matter is that even we have constraints to work within. I will explain further. The energies that we, the Source Entities, work with are essentially energy from the Origin. It IS the Origin's energy, and as such, we all have the same set of energies, the same building blocks, if you like, to work with. As a result, there are bound to be similarities. The similarities are based around the energies we are working with and how we combine them during our creation process. I will give a further example. The similarities that you find in the flora and fauna on your planet are because they are all created by using the same set of building blocks that you call DNA. Using DNA creates a finite set of physical vehicles,

140

some of which are similar, such as humans and apes, rats and mice, all of the fish species, all of the bird species. Commonality is everywhere as a result of the use of the same building blocks. Please note here that I have just been told by your Source Entity that there are many species that you have not catalogued yet, for some of them exist as semi-physical entities, and others have not yet been created as the permutations available are not anywhere near being used up yet. The universe is the limit in this instance. But let's get back to my environments.

I have created four main environments or universes, each consisting of the twenty-four dimensions and with 2,322 frequencies. Although Source Entity Two has four environments, this is only a similarity in division. And whereas other Source Entities have allowed all of their entities and their environments to be purely energetic, I have decided that all of my environments have what you would call a physical aspect to their appearance. This means that they have different levels of energetic cohesion, depending upon the dimension and frequency that is being experienced.

I see that you are thinking along the lines of your own physicality.

ME: *I have to admit that I am thinking along the lines that parts of the environment and its entities have a certain level of solidarity that is based upon frequency.*

Dimensions and Frequency

SE4: It is a reasonable example, poor but nevertheless useful in description. I will give you the concept in a way that you will be able to understand because there is a difference in how to understand dimension and

141

frequency.

As you rise through the frequencies, you move away from that which you experience at the previous frequency and start to experience that which is present in the new frequency. Using your own frequencies as an example, things like the desk you sit at (of a slightly lower frequency than you and, therefore, solid) will no longer be part of your new frequentic level. However, you will experience other things that are consistent with your experience or expectation of what a solid object, such as your desk is. This is because frequencies overlap to a certain extent, and you are still within a single dimensional continuum. Now if you consider a change from one dimension to another, then you have to consider a bigger picture—that of the dimension and the frequencies. When you move from dimension to another, you also move from one frequency set—one that is aligned with the former dimension—to the frequency set that is aligned to the new dimension. Although the number of these frequencies is the same (2,322), the characteristics can be different since some frequencies can be bigger or broader even when higher in nature.

ME: *Hold on. I thought that frequency was just that, frequency.*

SE4: No, frequency has more characteristics than just resonance for it also has the properties you would call magnitude, amplitude, and rotation. Your radio engineers know this and use it to some reasonable effect. Frequency also has the characteristics of spatial position, dimensional position, density, interaction—interconnectivity between different frequencies—and event position--time. All of these can change the modality of the frequencies being experienced and how they operate within a specific dimension. One thing is common though. The relationship between what is supposed to be solid—a solid will not pass through another solid if it is of the same frequency and modality—what is supposed to be non-solid but is in interface with solidity, and the energetic—that which is present in two or more frequencies concurrently. Then add that which is energetic and porous energetically— energies mixing will make a new composite energy if so desired.

ME: *So what you are saying is that what I am experiencing now in the physical would be duplicated in the next dimension to a certain extent—that extent being consistent with the relationships I have with the objects that surround me and the differences we have in frequency. However, this is not the case when I move up and down the frequencies because I will perceive objects of different frequencies going in and out of my perception as I move through these frequencies.*

SE4: With what you perceive being consistent with the range of the organs or energies being used as the tools for perception/detection; however, if your tools for perception are wide enough in range, you would still perceive objects of your old frequency even though you are in a new frequency. Yes, that is a reasonable summary and one that can be used in most of your dialogues with the Origin's Source Entities when referring to this subject.

ME: *So your environments have what I would call physical aspect to them?*

SE4: Yes.

ME: *Let me get this straight. The environments that you created only allow the entities you created to exist in the physical levels of frequency?*

SE4: Yes, but don't forget that the physical levels of frequency extend to a level much higher than those that you are currently experiencing. So although there are limitations—physical in nature—imposed on my entities, you in your current physicality would consider them as energy-based beings.

ME: *O.K., I think I understand what you mean. Then do they in their higher frequency environment have a universe that includes galaxies and solar systems with stars and planets?*

SE4: Not as you would recognize them. In your environment and resultant set of frequencies, you have a predominant shape for energy that has purpose, whether it is sentient or not. That shape is the sphere. In my environments the dominant shape for a large collection of energy is more like what you would call a doughnut.

The Doughnut Universe

ME: *A doughnut? Now you are playing with me.*

SE4: Not in the slightest. You see, the level of density in my environments dictates whether or not there is a center to the energy that collects to create what you know as planets. You are brainwashed into thinking that a planet needs to be a certain form. In essence, there is no dominant form for a planet—any form will suffice. Please note though that the form of a planet is based upon many factors that are beyond that which exist in the static frequencies. The doughnut form is common in my environments.

ME: *Do the entities that exist in these environments with doughnut ring planets work on the surface or inside the planet? Does it have a surface to live on or are they gaseous in nature?*

SE: They can be anywhere within the energy field that is created by the doughnut. That means they can exist on, within, or in the middle of the void centered within the area you may consider to be a solid mass. This center point would be the origin of the radius of the planet. This void is not truly void for it both contains energy and attractivity—what you might call gravity. It is this attractivity that keeps the planets shape the way they are.

ME: *I have just received an image of a ring magnet with the location and shape of the magnetic field superimposed on it. The field is a series of circles that go around the doughnut whilst also touching in the middle. No, they are interlaced in the middle. This appears to create another field that covers the whole doughnut shape. That can't be right. A magnetic field does not do that, at least not to my knowledge. It appears to be the same as both a ring magnet and a standard solid magnet.*

Figure 1: The Ring Magnet Image

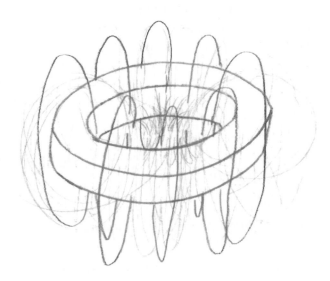

SE4: That's because you are not actually seeing a magnetic field in your image. What you have seen are the dominant lines of attractivity that surround and contain the energies that form the shape of the planet at its level of physicality/frequency.

ME: *So what entities live in the different areas? By this, I mean inside the solid, on the surface, or in the void?*

SE4: There is only one sort of entity, and it is able to adapt its form to whatever is best for the part of the planet where they like to exist—either in, on, or by it.

ME: *You said that they are physical. Are they metamorphs?*

SE4: As I previously stated, they are physical but not in your level/type/form of density. No, they are not metamorphs as you would describe or has been depicted in your science fiction books and films. They do modify themselves energetically to ensure they function at peak efficiency in the part of the planet they wish to inhabit. By creating their own field of attractivity, they draw those opposing energies that are necessary to allow what you recognize as a tactile response. The field is both personal to the entity and modulated to specifically attract the opposing energies.

ME: *Can you describe the form or shape of these entities?*

SE4: They have no specific form that you would recognize as a physical form because they change themselves to suit their local environment. However, if I was to describe the forms they have in a general sense, would that suffice?

ME: *Yes, of course.*

SE4: It would be relative to the doughnut-shaped worlds only.

ME: *That would be fine.*

Three Entities, Three Environments

SE4: The form the entities generally assume when in the central void area of the planet would be like a huge butterfly-type shape with the wings as accumulators of energies that allow their translation from point to point by using the lines of attractivity. They are very high in frequency.

The form they generally assume when on the surface of the planet is more like a heavier version of the butterfly form but with the wings deflated to the point of uselessness in a void environment. In this instance, however, the wings attract different energies that ensure that the entity is able to operate in a similar condition to you in a gravitational field. Other appendages also become visible for using energies and areas of physicality that cannot be handled by the deflated wings.

The form they generally assume when below the apparent surface of the planet—somewhat similar to the difference in air to water on your earth—is, therefore, a matter of creating a more streamlined form of the butterfly shape that has a repulsive field surrounding it. Its form would be a bit like crossing the surface-based form of the entity with a (Pause). I am thinking of using the word "fish," but the imagery is wrong. Let me search your memories further. O.K., I would like to use the word crayfish or crab but with significantly less density.

Figure 2: The Heavier Version of the Butterfly Form

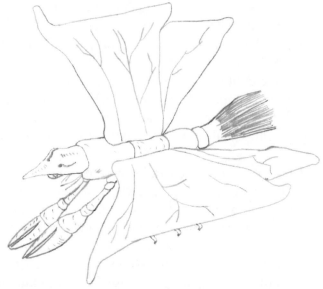

ME: *I am not sure I can get my head around this form factor.*

SE4: No, I can see that the description is woefully inadequate in your experience and language, but it will have to do. Suffice to say, the form they adapt is the most effective for existing in the environment inside these planets.

The Planets

ME: *Do these planets revolve around a sun?*

SE4: There is no need to have a local gravitational anomaly to attract and burn energies to create light and heat or all the other energies that are created in the combustion process that is the function of a sun.

ME: *Why is this?*

SE: We simply don't have the need for suns in my environments because light and heat is not required to either illuminate the universe or provide fuel or energy for those areas of local density that can be classified as planets. What we do have are areas where some of the planets of similar composition cluster together. You may call these galaxies if you like, but we don't have solar systems. In essence, we simply do not have the low frequency level that results in your sort of universal creativity, such as suns with planets rotating around them with solar systems that cluster together and rotate around themselves or create cloud-like formations. In a universe where heat and light are not required to sustain life, there is no need for a fire to create it.

ME: *I have just had another image in my mind of the planet you described to me. It appears to be all dark blue in the area of the doughnut that I would call solid. Would this be water?*

SE4: No, these planets do not have water. Water is a by-product of one of the most common elements you have in your universe, hydrogen. It is not available in my environments because the level of physicality is higher in frequency which negates its existence. Remember that material elements are a result of low frequencies. The fundamental law with frequency (across all Source Entity environments) is that the higher up the frequencies you go, the less material elements exist, and the more energetic elements exist.

ME: *So what is the blue appearance if it is not water?*

SE4: It is the visible representation of the major energetic element that makes up the planet.

ME: *Are you suggesting that these planets are primarily made up of one element?*

SE4: In general, yes, but the planet in your image also has some other elements. Your own planet is currently very physical in nature. As a result, it is made up of many low frequency elements—more, in fact, than any other planet in your universe.

The blue color is simply an emanation of that major element. It is also a product of the energies' response to

149

being worked with by the entities that exist on and within its energies.

ME: *So those three entities you described make the planet the color it is.*

SE4: As I stated before, it is a product of the major element and its reaction to being used by the entities that work with it.

ME: *Does the color change as a result of the purity of the work the entities do with the planet?*

SE4: Only in the intensity of the color. You can tell the level of entity and planetary evolution by the intensity of the color of the major element of the planet.

ME: *I have just seen an image of a group of planets, all glowing in brilliant colors. It is a beautiful sight.*

SE4: Yes, it is. That particular cluster of planets all have the same entities working with them in group harmony. They are evolving well, in both a planetary level and a group/individual entity level. I am pleased with them and their efforts.

ME: *I get the impression then that the planets are not solid in the sense that I know insomuch as the entities do not feel physical resistance when they work below the surface.*

SE4: No. There is what you call a surface tension that is at the interface between the surface of the planet and the inside part that is contained within the doughnut shape, and this is what some of the entities exist on. This is not to be confused with the crusty surface that your planet has. This is a relatively smooth surface and one that has little opportunity for other entities to exist on, such as trees or bushes. It does have other more mobile entities though, and these are entities created by those that exist in, on, or outside the planet's physicality but still within its energy field.

Mobile Entities—Living Cities

ME: *Tell me a bit about the mobile creations that the entities create that use the surface of the planet.*

SE4: They create areas where they can work together in the manipulation of energies to further create what you might call biological forms. Biological is not the correct term, but the concept is the same. By this I mean that the entities they create are designed to be self-sustaining energetically. To enable them to be self-sustaining, they need to be able to roam the planet's surface, so to speak, seeking areas where the energies they use are at their prime. These entities are singular and collective. The collective ones are usually much larger in size. They are seen as the areas where this planet's entities work within to further interact with the energies of the planet. It is for this reason that they are mobile, for they need to move themselves to the next location that is required energetically to support the work of the higher entities.

ME: *I have just received an image, and I thank you for all these images. They help a lot in my understanding of whole areas of what I can only describe as buildings, moving together to the next location. Wait a minute. The number of these buildings—they are of all shapes and sizes—is massive. It must be as big as a city in earthly terms.*

SE4: If you were to draw a comparison, then you would need to say that they are bigger than your biggest city on Earth. That is a true city, not including suburbs.

ME: *Can I use the description "living city" here, for that's what it looks like to me? It's as if the entities that created the buildings within the city created living beings within which they exist within, work within, and work with whilst also nurturing them as their own, like they are their children.*

151

SE4: They are their children to some extent, for they have created them. In doing so, they learn all about creation for a purpose and the responsibility of creation. Creation to achieve a purpose is one of the most powerful methods of achieving evolutionary progression. In this instance, the reason for creating the buildings and the resulting size of city is to harness and contain the energies that are being worked with. As each of the energies is refined to the point of requirement and usefulness, it is allowed to be mixed or exposed to the energetic products of another group of entities in another building. When the desired outcome of this larger mixing or manipulation of differing energy products is achieved, then that product is allowed to mix or be part of the product of other mixed or simultaneously exposed energies. This expansion is allowed to continue until all the buildings in the city are involved in creating one complex entity that is created for a larger purpose—that purpose being the final prerequisite for the development of a large, living, energetic organism.

ME: *And these large living cities move around the planet's surface to link up with the various energies that surround or are part of the planet's function.*

SE4: That's right.

ME: *So what is the overall role of these cities?*

SE4: They are used as guinea pigs by the creating entities to understand how to create life other than them. I will elaborate. The most important part of an entity's existence is the experience of creation, especially creation of things that have autonomy from the creator. This is true creativity. My entities work with the creation of structures to house certain energies. These are linked together to create interdependence of the structures and the energies they house. Together they create an entity in its own right, which if created correctly, is capable of continued existence through its own re-creation. During its existence it has to perform certain tasks which results in it gaining experience and ultimately mastery of these tasks. Interaction between the cities is also encouraged. It is the husbandry of these creations that gives my entities experience and evolution.

ME: *So my question on civilization is pretty meaningless then—because to work together on such projects requires the high level of interaction that is only possible with highly civilized entities.*

SE4: Correct. When you get to that level of civilization, everyone works in a naturally high state of harmony for the benefit of everyone with all working towards the end goal. Nobody is in it for itself, for all benefit equally.

ME: *So is that it? Is that all that this version of entities do— just work together to create larger autonomous entities?*

SE4: By and large, yes. Existence is not as complicated in my environment as it is in yours. Do not get me wrong though. The work that they do is not simple, for it is both a complicated and honorable task in itself. What I mean by your environment being more complicated is that you all operate in separation from each other, and, as a result, you do not work together in harmony. My entities are both separate and joined, and, as a result, they know what their roles are and the level of excellence they have to achieve to make the task they work on successful.

In terms of them being civilized, in their collective harmony, they achieve civilized function by being in harmony, for they work for the good of each other and the projects they work on. The infrastructure that you have for communication, transportation, and manufacturing that creates wealth allows further creation to support that infrastructure, and the individual is, therefore, not necessary.

ME: Hold on. I thought you said that they have cities, though? Surely you need infrastructure to support cities?

SE4: YOU called them cities, not I. Although cities are a reasonable description of them, they are not born out of the same need for localized trade and accommodation that yours are. They are born out of the need to create, experiment, and evolve so the need for personal properties, such as houses, cars, and trinkets are not required. I can see you frowning so I will explain a little more. Transportation is not needed because they stay within the group that is creating and controlling the project they are working on. Should they need to move from one place to another, they either move the whole city or use the energy lines on the surface of the planet to move. Personal energy is gained by aligning their own energies to those of the planet they are localized to, which, again, for those entities that are on the surface of the planet, is via the energy lines.

Inside the Planet

ME: What about those entities who are inside or under the planet's surface?

SE: They have similar tasks as those on the surface, but they use subtly different energies. Remember how I described their difference in form to you?

ME: Yes I do. They appeared to be similar in the doughnut's void and on the surface but different when inside or under the surface.

SE4: Yes, that is correct, but don't forget that they can translate from one form to another relative to the planetary area where they are working. This generally happens at the start or end of a project although some do change mid-project, but this is only when an entity's skills are needed to be updated/upgraded to help in its

154

project. An entity can only get those skills from a period of existence either in the void or below the surface or vice versa.

ME: *When I log into your universal environments, I see lots and lots of these doughnut-shaped planets. Do you have other shapes, and what is the shape relative to?*

SE4: There are other shapes, but they are not what you would recognize as a physical shape that could be attributed to a planet.

ME: *Wow! I have just received an image of a spiky ball-type shape. You can't be serious in suggesting that this is a bona fide shape for a planet in your environments?!*

SE4: Ha, ha, ha! You really are a stick in the mud. The shape of a planet or point of physicality for existence with-on or with-in does not need to be spherical like it is in your physical universe. Wait, I need to scan your memory that is that part of you in your real environment of energy. Ah yes, I see where the preconception is. It is based upon the standard form that is available to you in both your current physical environment that is in communication with me and that part of you that is energetic. You all naturally assume the sphere because it is both comfortable and makes the best use of your surface tension energies. Because your energies naturally form into the shape of a sphere, you naturally but incorrectly think that this is a universal standard that is used throughout the Origin's space and is also a dictate or universal law of physicality for the Source Entities as well. It may well be in your Source Entity's multiverses, but it isn't in mine—hence the shapes that you are seeing in your mind's eye. Don't forget that the physicality in my environments is nowhere near the same as what you are experiencing right now.

So, to answer your last question, yes, that shape is a bona fide shape for a planet in my environment;

therefore, I have shapes other than the doughnut-shaped planet that we have been talking about.

The Stickle Brick Planet

ME: We have only been talking about one universe and one specific planet in one of your universes What about the others? You must have many other civilizations doing other things to evolve.

SE4: Yes, of course. But you would never have enough time to discuss them in any detail as they are far too diverse and are far too different to that which we have just been discussing. In fact, I have selected the best example that I have that correlates to what you are capable of understanding, and I am capable of conveying to you with the language you have.

One of the things that you need to be aware of is that your existence on planet Earth is totally bizarre compared to almost all other entities in your Source Entity's environment, including what the other Source Entities and I have created. You think that because you exist in what you think is a quantifiable environment, you know it all. The problem is that what you experience is so far off the beaten track of what most entities experience that you have no idea what reality really is or could be. So when individuals, such as yourself, have the honor of being able to contact the greater reality and beyond, you tend to classify it into the pigeon holes that you know, and we have to work with that.

ME: O.K., I understand that is a limitation. So I guess that is why you have limited the information you have given me—so I could both understand and be able to convey it to the readers of this text when it is published.

SE4: Correct.

ME: *Taking this in mind and also taking into account that we are probably getting close the end of this dialogue (I was starting to sense that SE4 was starting to pull away now), what would be the evolutionary opportunities surrounding the use of the spiky planet I saw in my mind's eye? To me, it looked like a hedgehog all rolled up.*

SE4: In that particular instance, the entities that associate themselves with it work with the planet in a way that is particular to the needs of that planet. That planet type has a function that is specific to being in a community of planets—they stick together and work together as a whole.

ME: *Like a "Stickle Brick."* [Bristle Blocks—think of Lego with bristles instead of nubs and holes as connectors.]

SE4: Let me see . . . Yes! Like a Stickle Brick. The function of the entities is a symbiotic one where they guide the planet to the location of other planets of the same form factor. They then "plug" together to form a larger planet. When in this larger planetary configuration, they each have singular and collective functions. These functions affect the energies that exist within and around them. It is these energies that the entities use to create new planets of the same type. These new planets are then cast free for a period to allow them to gain their own energy profiles. They do this by attracting energies from their general environment. Depending upon location within my overall environmental area, the energies are different so the planets are allowed to move or be moved by the entities that assign themselves to the planet to the areas that they are attracted to. Call this their personality if you like. Once they are charged up with the energies they are attracted to and are able to use these energies for their own continued existence, they are then moved into a location where they may "plug in" to a group of similar planets, creating a bigger planetary entity.

157

Figure 3: The Stickle Brick Planets

ME: *This looks to me very much like a virus, growing by multiplication by division.*

SE4: Yes, I can see how you might think that; the process is somewhat similar, but that is where the similarity ends.

ME: *So why do these planets work in this way?*

SE4: You mean why do the planets and their entities do what they do?

ME: *Yes, that's what I meant.*

SE4: They do it to create planetary communities that have both the components of individual contribution and collective contribution whilst working with the smaller entities that work with them. Working together is one of the highest orders of work any entity can partake in. Within my environments it is an activity that is not reserved to smaller, higher power entities, such as you in your Source Entity's environments. It is there for all to work with, achieve, and experience.

Planetary Cooperation

ME: *A planetary community! Hold on. I can understand that planets are entities in their own right, but the idea that they can form their own communities is a bit beyond me.*

SE4: Why should it be? What do you think the galaxies are in your own universe?

ME: *My understanding of the function of galaxies in my universe is that they are entities in their own right with planets forming an integral part of them and their function as they have their own individuality.*

SE4: Correct. The difference in your universe is that the galaxies are the major entity with the planets and sun being components of that galaxy. In this particular instance it is the other way around. With the support of the smaller entities as assistants, the planets form communities by linking themselves together, the result is similar to a galaxy in your own universe, but the galaxy is not the entity. The planets are the entities. They are just grouped together. There is an interesting by-product of this linking together of planets though— coadunation, the linking together of smaller individual entities with individuality to create a larger entity that is the sum or exceeds the sum of all of the entities that are linked together. This results in an entity that is significantly more capable than the entity you call a galaxy, for the galaxy is the major entity made up of smaller parts. Whereas in this example the galaxy is a collective entity made up of small but major parts.

ME: *Whilst you were describing this concept to me . . .*

SE4: It was not a concept; it is a reality.

ME: *Right. Whilst you were describing this specific example of existence in your environment, I received an image of clusters or groups of planets—vast groups, groups as small as solar systems and groups as large as galaxies—but with them all linking together to form an even bigger entity, a super galaxy.*

SE4: And the super galaxies can merge together to create mega galaxies, and the mega galaxies can merge together to create super mega galaxies.

ME: *Wait, wait, now you're blowing my mind. Are you suggesting that these clusters or groups of planets can get bigger and bigger and bigger with no limit to how large they can get? Wait. I now see an image of an area full of small and large clouds with each cloud being a galaxy of linked planets. Some of these clouds are moving together to make bigger clouds. From my vantage point in this image, they look something like a huge nebula. Recognizing that nebulae are galaxies of a sort, the different parts of the nebula are different colors due to the different galaxies being of differing energies that are being worked with by the planets and the entities that work with each planet.*

SE4: Good summary. There is, of course, a limit to the size that a galaxy can become.

ME: *What is that? The total size of the environment they exist within and the total amount of energy associated with that environment?*

SE4: Well done. There comes a time where either all of the energy is used up, or the volume available is no longer available because it is full of energy created into entity.

ME: *So you are not infinite?*

SE4: No, of course not. I am the size that the Origin gave me when it created me. This is the same for all the environments that I created. These environments have both dimension and the various resources to go with that dimension. These are in the finite, not infinite although what I might call the finite, you might call the infinite; however, that is purely based upon your current perception of the greater reality. The difference is that the smaller entities that work with the planets are fully aware of their part in their greater reality.

ME: *I find it incredible to think that a whole environment can actually be filled by what would end up being one big nebula or super mega galaxy. What would be the purpose of a collective entity of such a size?*

SE4: In this particular instance, the purpose of becoming this size and using either all of the available energies in the creation process or all of the area available is to experience the effect on the greater entity—increased energetic facilities and growth through cooperation. That is, to experience the sudden limitation of such an expansion would be the evolutionary version of hitting a brick wall because with the decision to dissolve the merging, the larger entity would lose all the advantages that come with an entity of this size. The level of dissolution, being a collective decision based upon what level of individuality, is required to start the next set of experiences.

ME: *I see an image of a smoke cloud expanding to fill a clear balloon of known size. This smoke cloud then divides to become smaller clouds within this balloon. It then divides further to become speckles of dirty air—what I assume are small galaxies or clusters of solar system-sized collections of planets. Then it becomes a whole cloud again and finally becomes invisible. This last part I would guess is where the dissolution of the collective is right down to its lowest level of one planet and is therefore not visible.*

Figure 4: The Smoke Cloud in the Balloon Image

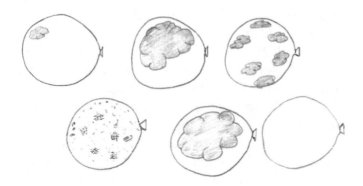

SE4: What you saw there is a very fast visualization of how this type of planetary cooperation develops or could develop. It is only a couple of examples of how it could develop but is good enough for this dialogue.

ME: So in a nutshell what you have shown me is that evolution is not just for the smaller entities but for the larger planetary entities as well. They can experience singularity or the various stages and sizes attributable to being linked together and cooperating to achieve a greater level of experience.

SE4: Yes, that would be a good summary. Remember that experience and evolution does not necessarily need complication. It only needs cooperation.

You have seen enough of my environments now. You need to rest a while and cleanse your energies before you move onto communicating with my colleague you will call Source Entity Five. Now go in peace and spread the word.

And with that my link to Source Entity Four was dissolved.

In Closing

When a Source Entity relinquishes its link with you, it results in a big change (loss) in energy/frequency, and this one was no different. There was, however, a couple of differences. I had been in contact with SE4 for longer than normal, longer than the other SEs to date. I had also been operating at a higher frequency than normal to ensure that the link was maintained, which was, to be perfectly honest, hard work. This was due to the vast differences in the concepts and the energies surrounding these concepts that SE4 was offering me, which ultimately needed to be filtered by SE4 to a level of understanding that I could both deal with and hopefully transcribe. To elaborate further, I had been on a high that was higher than normal, and I was now suffering from energetic cold turkey, especially when around the "everyday" people that I associate with. When I was with my wife and friends who are either spiritual or interested in such abstract metaphysical information, my energies were raised and the cold turkey was not so bad. It was a bit like going into a decompression chamber after a deep (SCUBA) dive. Quite clearly I was no longer grounded and needed to consolidate myself energetically before the next line of communication/dialogue, which would be with the Source Entity that I will refer to as Source Entity Five. As I was having difficulty operating in the physical world, I decided to raise my energies and contact my own Source Entity, the creator of our multiverse on this issue.

ME: *I need help here.*
SE: So I can see. But this was not unforeseen as we discussed this (privately) before we started this series of dialogues.
ME: *So what is happening?*

SE: Simply put, you are being stretched beyond your physically energetic limits. When you enter into a dialogue with another Source Entity, you create a link. This link is maintained throughout the period of time that the communication is planned to be over. That is not the few hours a week that you set aside for transcribing the information from these dialogues whilst in communication with the other SEs. It is the weeks or months that they are spread over. Establishing this link over this period of time is a necessary requirement, ensuring that you can continue the dialogue at a moment's notice without the rigamarole of intense meditative process. During this time you still maintain the link with me, and I have a different energy signature than the other SEs. This causes a conflict in energies, resulting in the tiredness you have been feeling even though I am giving you protection. In essence, your energies and frequencies are being maintained at a level well above the norm you are accustomed to, and, as a result, when you come down to just my energies, which are above your own, you still feel deflated.

ME: *So that explains the bags under the eyes.*

SE: Yes, to an extent. In support of this, you need to ensure that you are well rested and get as much sleep as possible.

ME: *Yes, I agree with you here as I have recently started to find that I need to have a quick half hour sleep after work.*

SE: That is your physical and energetic bodies telling you that they need to stabilize and balance the energies being accessed and used.

During the dialogues with the last four Source Entities, I was starting to notice an area of commonality. I was finding this a bit disturbing as a little voice in the back of my mind was saying that all I was doing was talking to the same entity—that

I was not really communicating with Source Entities other than my own but simply with one spiritual entity. I decided to offer this thought process to my own Source Entity.

ME: *Why do I get this feeling that I am talking to just one entity when I have identified with four to date?*

SE: Let me put your mind at rest. You are, indeed, communicating with different Source Entities. That is a fact. What you are experiencing though is the feeling of oneness that results from being so close to the Origin. Remember we are the first and only creations of the Origin. Everything else in the Origin's expanse is a product of Source Entity creativity and that includes your good self. When you consider that the modus operandi that we all have is to experience, create, and evolve, it is hardly surprising that there is a certain amount of continuity between the agendas of each of the Source Entities. If there was not continuity in this way, then there would be no point to our existence.

No, do not worry in this way.

What I can say though is this: the very fact that you are questioning the content that you are receiving gives it value. The process of questioning is both healthy and necessary. It is necessary because there is no way in the physical world you can prove that the content you are receiving is real rather than fiction. It is healthy because it helps you maintain your objectivity and your state of mind. These together validate the work, and validation is a necessary precursor to dissemination. It is validation that brings such information into the domain of the physical worlds.

ME: *Thank you that helps a lot. So this feeling I have of disappointment resulting in seeing continuity is also based upon the reduction in energies resulting from de-coupling from the other Source Entities.*

SE: In some part, yes. The fact that you also have a part of you that requires a certain type of information—an expectation derived from the physical existence you are currently experiencing. That information is either not available or is not relevant in these communications. In your own words, just accept.

ME: *Thank you. You help me a lot.*

SE: And I thank you for you have undertaken a most difficult task. Let us move on to the next Source Entity, Source Entity Five.

As these words were conveyed to me, I started to feel the change in energies that I had now come to associate with the protective energies that the Source Entity wraps around me when I enter into communication with the other Source Entities. I then felt the energy of the entity that was SE5. It was singular and accompanied with an image of a huge translucent ball of energy.

Chapter 5

Source Entity Five

I was wondering why I was getting this image of a singular entity when I felt its presence engulf me. I decided that I had better communicate with this presence as ignoring it would be an insult. It had, after all, made the effort to make contact with me, which it had no obligation to do.

ME: *Is that Source Entity Five?*

SE5: It is, and you have permission to refer to me as such, for it will make this communication easier.

ME: *Thank you. You may have been told by my Source Entity that I have a format that I like to use to start my dialogues, and then I just let the communication go the way it goes. I have been finding that this is the best way because trying to steer the questioning too much inhibits the flow of information, especially if the information is in variance with what I think I should be getting. Basically I have learnt to get myself out of the way and let you explain about you and your creation/s.*

SE5: That is a very wise thing to do and one that will stand you in good stead in this instance, specifically as I am singular. This is something that you have already sensed.

ME: *Yes, it is. I will, though, ask the standard questions about these items:*

- *your creation*
- *becoming aware*
- *experiencing yourself*
- *communication with the Origin*
- *what you are doing to evolve and help the Origin with its quest to know/understand itself better*

167

- *what you have created as a result*

SE5: I note that they are worded in a different way to the way you have written them in previous dialogues, but the content is still the same. I have already had some advice on what you might ask from my own communications with your Source, so I am aware of what routes you will be taking during our time together. In fact, we have, in essence, already had our dialogue; it's just that the part of you that is on the plane of existence that you are aware of has not yet been able to recognize it as happening. I think you know this aspect of reality, am I correct?

ME: *Yes. O.K., let's kick off with the dialogue as I am not aware of what my higher/real self has already done or is currently doing.*

SE5: Fire away.

Self-recognition

ME: *How and when did you become aware that you had your own thoughts—that you were sentient and had individual thought and recognition of self?*

SE5: It was actually a slow process for me. For a long time, what you would call trillions of your years, I was not fully aware that I was individual. What I was aware of was that I was part of a bigger reality, the Origin, but I did not know what the Origin was and what my relationship to the Origin was either. It was somewhat like what your babies experience during the first days of existence after being born.

ME: *So what made you become aware? Did the Origin have a hand in making you make the change from unaware to aware, or was it a gradual increase in awareness?*

SE5: It was a fully gradual process. My increase in awareness was based upon my increase in what you might call sensory experience.

ME: *What do you call sensory experience? For me, it is touch, taste, sight, and smell.*

SE5: For me, it was things that were interfering with my peripheral energies. In fact, it was the effect of the other Source Entities' creations brushing by me that made me realize that I had a periphery. It was a most disturbing experience. From this point onwards, my attention was set upon trying to understand what was causing this disturbance and how I could avoid the sensations that I was experiencing. As a result, I was drawn more and more into understanding that as I thought about not experiencing these sensations, they would go away, or the things that were causing the sensations would steer clear of my periphery or boundary. I even managed to create some thought processes that resulted in my catching those things that would try to invade or brush by my energies and hold them in one place whilst I looked into them with a view to seeing what they were. It was during the investigation into what one particularly interesting creation was doing, and why it was doing it that the realization that I was an entity capable of individual thought in my own right came to mind. This I found to be most interesting and decided to spend the next period of time creating independent thought and seeing if I could rationalize that thought by the justification of my own existence.

ME: *What do you mean by rationalization of independent thought by the justification of your own existence?*

The Power of Uncontrolled Thoughts

SE5: In my early recognition of self, I was unaware of the consequences of uncontrolled thought and what happens if thought goes unchecked.

ME: *Why do you need to check your thoughts?*

SE5: In the wider environment we call the Origin, every thought has the ability to lead to creation. As a result of my own unchecked thoughts, I was surrounded by thought junk—things that I had created but was not aware that I had created. Thought junk has an association with the creator of the thought. The association is such that the thought junk sticks to the creator of the thought in a random pattern in and around the energies of the creator. These thoughts are noisy and start to block out any thoughts that are being used in the communication process that I was later to have with the Origin and the other Source Entities.

ME: *How did you work that out?*

SE5: By noticing that the background thoughts I had been receiving were increasing and were duplicates of the thoughts that I had made before. I was quite literally being bombarded by my own thoughts and was being drained by the energetic associations that these thoughts were making.

ME: *How can a thought drain you of energy?*

SE5: By the sheer fact that they start to gain an impetus of their own, especially thoughts created out of Source Entity or Origin energy.

ME: *Impetus?*

SE5: A snowball effect that results in the thought gaining more energy the longer it remains in existence. If left unchecked or not recovered by the originating entity, a thought can quite literally become as large as the creating entity and even take it over.

ME: *Surely this can't happen to an entity as small as me.*

SE5: You are made from your Source Entities energy?

ME: Yes.

SE5: Then it can happen to you as well.

This was a complete surprise to me—that we as individual and independent entities were capable of literally covering ourselves in stray thoughts that clouded our already limited connectivity to our higher/real selves and further isolated us in the physical existence, one we believe is our only existence. It did, however, made perfect sense. I was even able to recognize some aspects of stray thought junk on my own aura. I cleared them away with a single thought and felt a shiver going down my spine and my skin tingle as my aura's functionality returned as a result of it being clear again.

In my mind's eye I saw a crowd of people. All of the people had their auras covered in various types and levels of sticky thought-based stray energy. Due to their own longevity without being cleared out, some were starting to both gain a level of individuality and had gained the ability to suck the energy out of the person that created them from their own stray unchecked thoughts—thoughts that were capable of significant levels of creativity if only the person that owned them knew how to use that facility properly.

SE5: That's a very good example of what was happening to me. The only issue was that I am significantly bigger than you, and I was also totally covered in these thought forms. As an example, if you were to consider my basic normal form as a sphere, then when I noticed what was happening to me, my external form was that of a sphere covered in random odd-shaped creations.

ME: I have just seen an image of a dragon-shaped entity slithering over you. What is the significance of that? It seems a strange piece of imagery to have.

SE5: I sent you that because it illustrates two things: first, that the thought forms are insidious; and second, that they were of such energy that they were able to create their own form at will. They were, in fact, their own entity—individual in every aspect. Except one, that is.

ME: *What was that?*

SE5: Because they were created by me, they were contained (held) by my energy and, as such, needed to stay with me to continue to exist. They were like . . .

ME: *I have just received an image of a snake pit with thousands of snakes crawling over each other, each one looking for its own space.*

SE: I was going to use the words "the entities you call snakes in a bucket," but you beat me to it. I was literally infested with them.

ME: *Did the Origin offer you some help or advice?*

SE5: No. At that point, I was not at that level of awareness, and the Origin had not yet decided to make itself known to me. In essence, this part of my existence was fully of my own doing and ultimately was part of my own evolutionary existence. It was essential training in being careful about what I thought and how I thought about what I was thinking. But getting back to the one exception.

ME: *Yes, what was it?*

SE5: The fact that I created these thoughts and the thoughts were of my own energy meant that I had ultimate control over their existence. Once I recognized this fact, it took less than a nanosecond to clear them away.

ME: *How did you do that?*

SE5: By simply re-absorbing their energy back into my own. Don't forget that they are my energy, and, as such, my energy is under my control. As a result I could and can do anything I wanted to do with them.

ME: *Including destroying them?*

SE5: Destroying them would have resulted in me losing the energy.

ME: *I didn't think energy would be lost.*

SE5: Energy cannot be lost, per se, but it can be lost by the individual. Lost energy does not mean that it is gone forever; it simply means it is lost from the entity that had it in the first place.

ME: *So where does it go?*

SE5: Back to the Origin. Don't forget that the Origin created the Source Entities from its own energies; it gave up those energies to create us. Based upon that, any energy that we destroy doesn't actually destroy the energy. It destroys the association of the energy with the entity that was authorized to use it. The association of energy is the link energy has with the entity it was assigned by the Origin.

ME: *So would I be right in saying that you would be giving up part of yourself if you destroyed this stray thought energy.*

SE5: You would, and although it is not what you would call a sin to do so, it is not in our best interests as it ultimately limits our energetic mass and, therefore, our ability to create.

ME: *So what did it feel like to suddenly have all this energy back and have your communicative abilities restored as a result of clearing away your stray energy?*

SE5: It was like you feel when you return back to your energetic self, when you give up the heavy suit of your physical vehicle. Elation!

What's more, this was part of a defining moment for me, as it was during this time that I realized that I was an entity capable of independent and original thought. The thought forms created by my unchecked thinking were proof of this. This started a period of experimentation in what you call philosophical thinking. This also expanded my consciousness and led me to the later opinion (after my communication with the Origin) that I was best employed in my particular role of helping the Origin understand itself better by remaining in a singular configuration.

ME: *What does that mean?*

SE5: I meant that I decided that I would not create any other entities to help me perform my task.

ME: *Wait a minute. That ties in with the feeling I had when I first logged into you, that you were singular.*

SE5: That's right, and that feeling that you had was because you did not detect any other entities that were associated with me—hence, the feeling of singularity.

Developing Awareness

ME: *Let's elaborate on this subject for a bit longer. It is one of the subjects that I have discussed with all of the Source Entities I have contacted so far.*

SE5: As I said, this was a defining moment for me. Suddenly realizing that I WAS, was amazing. Let me put this in context for you. I had just removed all of the thought forms that surrounded me, slowing me down, masking me from the reality of my existence and what was existing around me. I had become used to this condition; I was in it for millennia. It was like being blind and then being able to see. But this was not just being able to see; it was being able to see, understand, and relate to self, myself. This gave me a datum to work from. I recognized myself as an individual entity in my own right. I was surrounded by other entities, entities that were similar to me. Each of these entities was at a different state of realization, of evolution, of experimentation. I felt an affinity with them. We were all the same, and we had a job to do.

Then there was the Origin.

I noticed that one of the entities that I was aware of was in communication with something that I could not perceive. All that I could *see*, if that is the right word, was a sort of tube linking the entity, a Source Entity with what appeared to be a "skin" that surrounded us all. The tube changed in appearance as the communication progressed.

ME: *What changes in appearance did you see?*

First Conscious Contact with the Origin

SE5:   Its size and shape changed as well as the color, dimension, and frequency. It even sparkled at times. It was truly beautiful to behold. The Source Entity being communicated to reciprocated the form, dimension, and frequency in tune with the tube and its communication process. I even noticed that the area of "skin" surrounding the tube also had an appearance similar to that of the tube. I then looked around and saw that, on the odd occasion and over a period of time—I use the word *time* here just to explain that I saw this happen separately and not altogether or instantaneously—that this tube or a tube connected with several of the other Source Entities for a period of communication after which their appearance changed totally. I queried within myself why this was in separation and not altogether in totality and why the Source Entities changed. At this point I also had a sudden connection with the "skin" via a tube. I had made my first contact with the Origin.

ME: *What did that feel like, the first contact, that is?*

SE5:   I can only describe it as awesome. I suddenly knew who and what I was for sure. I was one of the twelve entities that a larger entity, an entity that was energy with sentience, had created in order to fully understand itself better. It had given up part of itself to create us, the twelve Source Entities, and the creation in itself was part of an experiment that it was running within its "self" to see how others would become aware and gain sentience, as indeed it had. It was seeing if a lesser content of energy would result in lesser beings.

ME: *And did it result in the creation of lesser beings?*

SE5: No. In fact, one of the conclusions that the Origin came to was that the content of energy did not specifically result in the generation of lesser beings. I learned that we had all of the abilities of the Origin and that was one of the things that the Origin was trying to understand.

ME: *But surely you cannot be equal to the Origin? You are a creation of the Origin.*

SE5: That is true, but the Origin gave us exactly the same energies that it was composed of, including all of the interpretations of those energies.

Interpretation of Energies—A Möbius Loop

ME: *Interpretations of energies? That's a new one on me!*

SE5: Energy has a different interpretation depending upon the dimension it is within and the frequency within that dimension, not forgetting, of course, that the energy itself IS the dimension and frequency.

ME: *What? How can energy be the dimension and the frequency when it is within the dimension and has frequency? You have just turned everything I know, or think I know, upside down.*

SE5: Yes, maybe, but it is a fundamental piece of physics that energy is within and without dimension and energy. It permeates all that is.

ME: *But that's like saying that the outside of a tennis ball is the inside of a tennis ball and vice versa.*

SE5: Correct and everything in between is the surface as well. Everything that IS, IS.

176

ME: *O.K. I will have to leave that one for the moment.*

SE5:   No, you don't need to. You have a concept that I can show you to help you understand. You have the Möbius loop, do you not?

ME: *We do.*

SE5:   And the Möbius loop can be used to explain the fact that a surface can be both inside and outside, can it not?

ME: *Yes, it is quite a good model; it can be explained mathematically as well.*

SE5:   Good. Then you consider that in your representation the Möbius loop is a two-dimensional representation of a surface in a three-dimensional environment.

ME: *Go on.*

SE5:   You said that this can be explained mathematically and as such can be used to explain a plane in a space.

ME: *O.K., I'm still with you.*

SE5:   Then all you need to do is expand your thought process to include the fact that "surface" is merely a representation of form.

[I was going to use "dimension" here, but it didn't make sense. SE5 changed it to "form" as it better represented what it was going to say next].

Energy has no form. It just IS, and, as a result, it can be considered as multi/omni-form simply because it has no form. It is formless. As a result, that which can be within a plane or dimension can also be without. The plane or dimension which includes frequency is the energy, and the energy is the plane, dimension, and frequency, all concurrently.

I wasn't sure whether this explanation of energy being inside and outside of dimension and frequency was correct, especially as it suggested that energy was a fundamental component of itself, a somewhat convoluted conundrum of the chicken and egg variety. I am sure that physicists who read this text may like to disagree. One thing is sure though: this is the explanation I received from Source Entity Five, and I am sure that it may be in total variance to the currently acquired human knowledge on this subject. I welcome anyone to offer a mathematical space model on how this can or cannot be. Undoubtedly, the process of proving such an explanation will expand mankind's understanding of this concept of reality. The glove of challenge is well and truly thrown on the ground.

Equality in Creation

ME: So let's get back to the communication you have with the Origin and the creation of beings with lesser energetic content whilst still being equal to the Origin.

I find this a little bit hard to understand. How can an entity that has a smaller volume of energy and energetic content be equal to the Origin? It makes no sense to me. Surely a lesser being, albeit only lesser in content could not be considered equal. Or was I missing something, something fundamental? I would have to see what Source Entity Five had to say on the matter.

SE5: Humanity has a very bad habit—the need to compare others with its self and its own level of understanding.
ME: I guess we do. I also guess that we are not very good at it either.
SE5: You certainly are not, and acceptance is something you should embrace as a race. It will make you calmer.

Because I can see that you are chomping at this particular "bit," I will try to describe to you the fundamentals surrounding creation, especially creation in equality and creation in terms of function. Then we will return to what I discussed with Origin.

Creation is one of the most honorable things that an entity can do, for creation is a fundamental platform towards experiencing evolutionary progression. There cannot be evolution without creativity. This is a universal law, one of the first things that the Origin imparts to us when we achieve the level of awareness required to invoke the first communication opportunity with the Origin.

To create in equality is to create without fear—fear that the creation will be "better" than the creator. This is nonsense, for the whole objective surrounding creativity is to experience more than is currently being experienced. This is especially so when the creator is creating an autonomous entity, for to create inferiority is to be inferior in creation, and this cannot be so.

ME: *So how can an entity, an autonomous entity, be considered equal if it is not of the same size dimensionally and, therefore, energetically?*

SE5: It is created in equality and as a result. it is equal. The energetic *size*, for want of a better word, is not a component of equality, for size does not specifically affect the ability to evolve. Take yourself as an example. Energetically you are smaller than I am by several magnitudes of dimension, frequency, and energy. But you are nevertheless in equality even if you are created by one of my peers. Your abilities may be limited to the constraints resulting from the amount of energy you have currently available to you, but in reality you are able to draw upon all of the energy that is freely available within the environment that your Source Entity has created if you so wanted. If you had enough imagination, you could, in fact, create an environment as large and as capable energy-wise as that created for you all to exist in by your own Source Entity. Your limitation is only in your own thinking, not in your

179

ability. Of course, you do have limitations, and those only exist when you have reached a point that is constrained by the boundaries that the Source Entity has itself, or you simply cannot perceive anything more expansive. Your Source Entity has given you all—that is, the countless billions of you that it has created, the same level of opportunity that it had. I am aware that the Source has given you a figure, but when you incarnate, you don't do it in singularity; you are in multiplicity. In this instance you are all in equality.

What I will say though is that there are entities that are created out of a need for pure functionality. These are also created out of equality, but they are not endowed with the freedom of ability that an entity, such as you/mankind in energetic representation, are given. They are created to perform certain tasks and those tasks alone.

ME: *Hold on here. I would classify these entities as lesser beings.*

SE5:   They are not lesser beings. They are beings created in equality with a singular purpose—that purpose being their role within the environment they were created to exist within.

ME: *So what would such a role be?*

SE5:   You should know this, for you have already discussed it with your own Source Entity.

ME: *Are you talking about what we call galaxies?*

SE5:   A galaxy would be considered as a large entity in your environment, would it not?

ME: *Yes.*

SE5:   Would you consider a galaxy as an entity of lesser importance or ability?

ME: *No, how can it be? It's massive compared to my own physical size.*

SE5: But it has a singular function. It is not free to access all of the energies that entities of your type can. It does not have the level of creativity that entities of your type have. You have no limits except those that you place on yourself.

ME: *You're suggesting that a galaxy is a lesser entity then. No, I will re-phrase that. A galaxy is an entity that is of function of singular purpose, whatever that may be.*

SE5: Yes, and in your environment it is to gather stray energy and create areas that can be used for evolutionary experience in the physical and surrounding frequencies or dimensions. That is all they are employed for. They have no other role. Even though they have no other role, they were still created in equality. Equality is given because their role is important.

ME: *So what you are saying is that in the eyes of the creator, the created is held in equal consideration simply because it has an important job to do. If that job wasn't necessary and important, it would not have been created in the first place.*

SE5: Correct. And don't forget all things that are created are of equal importance. Whatever its ability, everything in creation is assisting the Origin in its task of furthering its awareness of self. In itself, this ensures evolutionary opportunity for the Origin, for even the Origin needs to evolve.

Expansive Oneness with Origin

Throughout my communications with the Source Entities, I had noticed that on a number of occasions the direction that I wanted to go was ultimately diverted by the Source I was communicating with in order to expose me to another subject. In hindsight, the subject matter was obviously very relevant. This was one of those occasions. Although I was very aware that I should take information as it comes and not over-steer the dialogue, I endeavoured to get back on track.

ME: *So let's get back to the first contact you had with Origin. You were saying that, as with each of the first communications with the Origin you had witnessed, you were suddenly attached to a multi-colored, multi-frequential tube that was also connected to some sort of outer skin. This skin presumably was the Origin itself.*

SE5: Correct. The communication was instantaneous, complete, and concise. As you are already aware, I was given the full suite of information about my/our creation, the need for our creation, and the roles we were about to start. It was fascinating to understand that the Origin itself had been in solitary existence for many, many millennia! I appreciate that you know there is no such thing as time, but I need to give you the information using concepts that you will be able to understand. Therefore, the period that passed during which the Origin had existed in sentience before making the decision to create twelve equal entities as mirror images of itself can only be relayed to you in terms of time. This would be best recorded as billions upon billions of what you call years, the period of existence you use to describe the rotation of the physical aspect of the local density you work with in a three-dimensional condition—the earth around the energy singularity you call the sun.

ME: *Yes, I guess that the story is the same in terms of the roles you all have to play in the Origin's plan for the understanding of self and the evolution of self. What I would really like to know is what the dialogue was that was specific to you, that only you had with the Origin, and that did not include the other Source Entities and your collective roles.*

SE5: There was very little in what you would call dialogue specific to my role because the general rule was that we had freewill to do whatever we wanted to achieve the task at hand. And by freewill, I mean freewill. We had no rules within which to work. It really was "suck it and see." What I did was ask what the other Source Entities were doing or were planning to do to achieve further enlightenment, as I was eager to ensure that I did not do the same thing. You will notice that the other Source Entities you have communicated with have a theme of creating environments and populating those environments with smaller more nimble entities, each with a set of rules or goals to work within. I did not want that as I felt that at that point in my existence I could achieve what I wanted to achieve by being singular in state.

ME: *What was it like to be connected to the Origin in such a positive way?*

SE5: It was like I was the Origin, which essentially we all are. But when you are given the gift of individuality and then are re-exposed to a coadunate state, it is like nothing you have ever experienced before. You experience a similar level of, shall I say elation, when you are back with your prime energies—that which is the real you in totality and not just that which is projected into the physical. You feel whole again.

I can see that you are trying to find another example to explain this conditional change.

It would be like living in a 10 x 10 cabin and then suddenly being able to live in the biggest mansion you could ever imagine. It would be like being constrained within a single room—that room representing an aspect of your "self"—and suddenly you have many many many rooms. Think of each room representing an aspect of you that you have been cut off from and each corridor being a link to an aspect and the functional memory of that aspect. Then think of that aspect having many different corridors that can be used to access it, some of which include the multiple use of aspects to achieve what you need to achieve.

ME: *If I was to associate a room with each of your aspects, how many rooms would you have?*

SE5: Countless. And this was the problem that the Origin had. It simply did not know how many aspects of self it had. And this was one of the reasons we were created. To establish how many aspects of self the Origin had. We do this by trying to experience and, therefore, establish how many aspects of self we have as Source Entities. This then feeds back in to the task that the origin gave us. You can imagine what that means, can't you? I was suddenly plugged into a resource that was simply too big to even start to comprehend. It was literally awesome to the point of paralysis [ME: That would explain why, in my visualization of the Source Entities communicating with the Origin via the tube, they appeared to "freeze" momentarily]. As a result of this revelation, I was also able to understand that the part of the Origin that I was in contact with was but a microcosm of the whole. The Origin had limited that part of itself that was in communication with me to a level where it would not overpower me with pure expansiveness. It would be similar to me giving you access to all that is me. In your current condition, it would send you quite mad. Your consciousness would get lost in the expansiveness.

ME: *The Origin must do the same when it is in contact with me then.*

SE5: Correct, and in comparison, that part of the Origin that is in contact with you when you communicate with it is a fraction of that which is the Origin that is in contact with me when I contact it. In this instance, it really is all about size and what you can cope with as a result of your size—*size* being your level of expansiveness in this instance. But don't forget, size is not a measure of equality for we are equal to the Origin.

ME: *I get the impression that you came to some sort of agreement with the Origin in terms of what you wanted to do in your role as Source Entity.*

SE5: No so much an agreement but an understanding. Once I had calibrated myself to the vast wealth of information that was available to me during my connection to the Origin, I was able to understand what was already known by the Origin and those Source Entities that had already contributed to the cause. I was, therefore, able to create my own plan to contribute, the bones of which I shared with the Origin and which I am now in the process of delivering.

ME: *I would be very honored if you would take the time to share with me that plan and how you have achieved some of its aspects.*

SE5: That we can start in our next communication.

A Singular Entity

ME: *One of the things that I find interesting is that you are a singular entity. Everything I feel about you when I log into your energy is "singular." This is a really strange feeling, specifically because when I compare the feelings I get when I log into the other Source Entities, it is so different.*

SE5: What you feel with the other Source Entities when you are in communication should not be compared with me. May I explain what you are experiencing when you log into the other Sources?

ME: *Yes, please. I would be interested to know.*

185

SE5: The difference is that you feel connectivity through collectivity; I think you know this as coadunation, the creation of a bigger being through the connection of smaller independent beings together in unison with the desire to be in unison. This feeling is like tapping into myriad neurons, each with a job to do that results in a collective output. It's a bit like the transistors in one of your microprocessors. When you connect with me, you do not get this feeling—a feeling of expansion through connection because all you get is me. If I had created a number of smaller beings to help me with my work, you would have received the same feeling as that which you feel when connected to the other Source Entities.

ME: *So why did you decide to be a singular entity in your work? Surely it would have been more efficient to maximize your investigation through multiplication?*

SE5: That would have been the common thing to do. Shortly after my first communication with the Origin, I was in full understanding of the work that had been done to date by the other Source Entities with all but one other re-creating themselves. The other you know as Source Entity Twelve, the Source Entity that is still to become fully aware.

ME: *I was thinking about that Source Entity. Is communication with it possible?*

SE5: That is not for me to say, but I will tell you one thing: you will need the help of the Origin to even try to consider such an act. You had best wait until the end of your other communications before starting such an undertaking, for we will all be observing. No-Thing has tried to communicate with it yet, not even the Origin.

ME: *O.K., I will leave that to later then. Let's continue to discuss your plan.*

SE5: The plan I had did not include my division into smaller entities. I had seen that the others had started along this line of self-discovery, but I decided that I would work

186

on a more introspective method. This did not include multiplication or division.

ME: *This must slow down your ability to work on what and who you are.*

SE5: Only in so much as I am not dealing with the minute detail that can be achieved by the creation of smaller entities, such as you.

ME: *This sounds like you kept your investigations to a higher level of frequency and dimension.*

SE5: Indeed. More importantly, I am experiencing things first hand and not through a smaller creation that is designed to represent me.

Now the plan I agreed upon with Origin—my plan was simple: to continue my evolution by introspective evaluation of self through experimentation and creativity on myself.

ME: *That seems a bit like changing yourself and seeing how it feels.*

SE5: You are not far from the truth. The objective was and is to create things that directly affect me and to experience/understand how those things that affect me change my function.

ME: *Do/did you ever get to a point where a creation you made was irreversible? For example, did one of the creations you made ever affect you in such a way that you could not reverse the effect?*

SE5: No, never. One of the things I do when I create is to put a limit on the existence period of whatever I have created. So in the event that I create a condition that results in me totally losing control, which has happened by the way, I return to full functionality when the life of the creation is over. Even in full loss of control, I am able to record the experience and memorize it. Total loss of control is an interesting thing to experience for a Source Entity.

ME: *I am receiving an image of complete mayhem. Was this a result of your experience of being out of control?*

SE5: Yes, it was. The image you are receiving is things being created and un-created. My extremity being manipulated, stretched, squeezed, warped, dimensionally rotated, manipulated, undulated, and spliced is but a small example of what happened to me in that period of creation. If I were to give you a visual representation, it would appear to be a bucket of snakes with each snake eating, being eaten, or being created (reproduced) by themselves and their counterparts concurrently. As an experience, it was most interesting as environmental conditions—this is me creating an environment within myself—were created that I would never have considered possible to be worthy of creation. Such an example would be the spliced undulation of dimension. This results in dimensions within and without dimension. In your current understanding of dimension, the dimensions are separated and are inflated with frequential energies. In this instance, there was no frequency-based inflation of the dimensions because the dimensions were inflated by dimensions, and these dimensions were also present in other dimensions. It was like everything existed within and without all at the same time. If I were to describe this as an environment, I would only be able to use the word conundrum in its description of function. Furthermore, as an environment that could be used as an area to house smaller entities, it would have failed because no energy would have existed.

ME: *Hold on. I thought that energy could not be destroyed, only converted.*

SE5: Energy needs frequency to exist, and if there is no frequency, there can be no energy. If there is no energy, there can be no entity and without an entity there is no life—at least no life that can be quantified in any descriptive way that you would understand.

ME: *Try me. I am very open-minded.*

SE5: O.K. In this instance the dimensions themselves gained sentience. They were intelligence without frequency and energetic content. It was a new form of . . . *material* . . .

ME: [This took a long time to come to me as a descriptive word, for how do you put a word to something that is effectively above and beyond dimension, frequency, and energy?]

SE5: . . . from which to work and create. It was just as well that I have a function that records and memorizes the conditions experienced, so I can reproduce it whenever I require.

ME: *Hold on. Are you saying that the dimensions themselves without the energies and frequencies to inflate them became sentient in their own right?*

SE5: Correct. You see, one of the things that you have not been exposed to in your communications is the possibility for dimension to become sentient. You are aware that you, as energy, are sentient.

ME: *Yes.*

SE5: Then it should not be a great step forward to understand the simple concept that frequency can also have sentience.

ME: *I take your word for it. In this instance, I would expect that this is entirely possible. Can I offer my level of understanding?*

SE5: You may.

ME: *Here's my understanding at this point. Energy can have sentience because it has an environment that sustains its existence that is called dimension and frequency and that that inflates dimension. Frequency can also have content, such as the lower frequency content of radio, microwave, light, or radiation. It is this content that humankind has only just managed to exploit and use for the transmission of information.*

SE5: There are many, many other forms of content that can be used that are not tied down to the physical and that you have not even considered or dreamt of in your science fiction. Many of these would make your existence even easier, I would suspect, than it currently is, by using frequency as a tool.

ME: *O.K., because frequency has content, it can also develop sentience. Because it is part of dimension, it is contained. The dimension allows it to grow. I have a problem here though as the only thing I can relate to as dimension given sentience is you, a Source Entity.*

SE5: Although Source Entities are dimension, frequency and energy combined we can separate them all out to exist as individual content in their own right. If I were to categorise the three then I would suggest that dimension was the highest and energy was the lowest. Dimension can have individualisation and therefore sentience because it is the highest of the components that make us all up, including the Origin.

Dimension is very misunderstood in your level of existence, for you think of it as an environment, a continuum, that is purely down to your size and position within the hierarchy that the Origin and your Source Entity have created. Left to its own devices, any object/thing can gain sentience given a long enough period of existence in one state. Yes, I heard your thoughts—so can and do rock and minerals. Dimension is just a higher form of existence and, therefore, sentience. Of course, it is like no-thing you as mankind has ever experienced or will experience in your physical state.

ME: *But isn't a continuum a low level environment, one that is just above the third dimension, what we call space-time?*

SE5: Correct. But in this instance there is only one environment that can be called a continuum—one that involves dimension, frequency, energy and the recognition of the passage of events, time—which is where you are right now. A parallel dimension of equal content could be classified as a continuum but only if it has the full complement of the four components specified above. None do in YOUR universe. You need to be in a "multiversal" environment to have this effect take place, and it will only take place if your Source Entity requires it as a function of its environmental creation. This would be classified as a parallel universe and not a continuum. The universe you exist within does not have parallel content, at least not in what you would consider parallel. The only parallel content would be the dimensions, frequencies, and energies—not that which occupies it.

ME: *So why do our scientists talk of such possibilities?*

SE5: Because they remember memories of their energetic existence or are subconsciously tapping into the multiversal mind that they are part of. As I stated before, a continuum requires a multiverse to exist. There is only one continuum per universe—those that are classified as the physical levels. The content of such continuums would NOT be parallel. There simply is no need for the effects that a parallel continuum could offer since they are finite in comparison to the timeless environment that is the norm of any multi-dimensional universe that is above the first three.

Ah! I see the conundrum you have now. You (mankind) are thinking of alternative realities all existing at the same time and getting them mixed up with the word "continuum." Alternative realities are NOT continuums. It is the myriad of events that crisscross each other, depending upon how you may or may not react to a certain set of events. Each minor change to the way you

191

act or react causes a different chain of events to take place. This can only work in the higher dimensions of a multiversal environment, where the majority of your energetic content exists right now. The alternative reality is just that—an alternative to what currently IS, and that involves all of the entities that you are and interact with. Hence, there is possibility of meeting an alternative YOU in an alternative reality if you choose to work on two or more realities at the same time, which incidentally most of you already do. In this instance, each alternative YOU is playing out in a simultaneous fashion each alternative that is possibly available to you given the range of possible actions/reactions to a particular event. This does not happen in a continuum because you are limited to the lowest physical dimensions.

I can see that this has not answered your question on how a dimension can have sentience.

ME: *No, it doesn't, but it does answer other questions.*

SE5: I will try to answer this question in a succinct fashion then. Dimension can develop sentience without the other content of energy and frequency simply because it is a higher function of the Origin's make-up. Dimension is not something that we as Source Entities create. It is something that we can manipulate because it is a higher function of the Origin's make up and is, therefore, a higher function of our own composition. A Source Entity can separate dimension into smaller levels or layers capable of holding and supporting higher and higher energies and frequencies. However, that/those dimension/s can and do become sentient in their own right. Sentience is awareness of self, as you are aware, but sentience does not necessarily mean that you can affect the condition or the environment you are in. Consider the bird you call a parrot. It is aware of self, as is a monkey, but neither of them is fully sentient.

ME: *Our scientists would argue that the monkey and the parrot are not sentient.*

SE5: They both are sentient, but they are sentient on a low level—one that means that they are not able to change themselves and their environment.

ME: *Are you suggesting that dimensions are on the same level of sentience as the parrot and the monkey?*

SE5: No, they are a quantum leap apart, but in the scale of things, they are in similarity. For instance, the difference in sentience between you (in your current state) and the parrot and the monkey is similar but at a different magnitude to that difference between dimensional sentience and the sentience that a Source Entity has. In dimensional sentience the dimension is aware of itself and its function within the greater environment that it finds itself within. That is all it needs to have. However, a dimension can change itself to a certain extent in order to ensure that it creates the optimal environment for frequency and energy should it desire to be occupied as such.

Reasons to Remain Singular

I have to admit to being unprepared to talk to Source Entity Five on the subject of dimensional sentience. This is primarily because I wanted to discuss more about what it has achieved since its creation and awareness of self. In reality though, such a dialogue is interesting in its own right. I am starting to think that any "thing" that is created from the correct material (from the Origin) can become sentient; however, this bit on dimensions being sentient or capable of being sentient throws one off-track a little though. But then again, the whole point of communicating with the Source Entities was to gain as much information as possible whilst keeping it within the realms of what would be considered understandable on the human level. Based upon this, the best and only route forward is to just go with the flow and accept the little diversions in direction as they happen as being both necessary and timely in terms of the information being received. It is wise to note that the communication sessions that any channeler has are not about the channeler but about what is important for the human race to be exposed to at this particular point (in time?). It is also wise to have some limited but healthy challenging of the information being received to assist in the process of validating what has been received. We don't want to over-challenge the entity that we are communicating with since it would both stop the flow of information and make the entity wonder if the channeler is worthy of being used as a channel, but we do want to be certain that what we receive is pure to the purpose. It was at this point that I decided to push on with the task of understanding Source Entity Five's reasons for staying singular. After all, this would be good experience for me, as I was aware that there was one other Source Entity that was still singular, the one that the Origin had told me about whilst I was writing "The History of God" that had not yet become self-aware. On that thought I carried on with the dialogue with Source Entity Five.

ME: *O.K., here's the big question: why or what made you decide to stay singular?*

SE5: I simply saw what was happening around me and decided to create for myself, within myself, that which was necessary for my own evolution and expansion of my knowledge. It was quite clear to me that I was experiencing more than was necessary to sustain my existence from an evolutionary perspective without the need to gain a greater level faster by using the divisional methods used by the others.

ME: *Before I home-in on the reasons why it was so clear, can you elaborate on the need to sustain your existence? I thought Source Entities were to all intents and purposes immortal. I mean created for eternal existence.*

SE5: We are to a greater extent, but it is a wise entity that notes the fact that the Origin may decide to remove that gift from us if it so chooses. I know for a fact that right now, the Origin is immensely pleased with the performance of all its creations and all that they have created/experienced to further their evolution and, therefore, has no thoughts of changing what it has created in any way, shape, or form.

ME: *But why would the Origin change what it has created to another model of creativity if it is successful in what is happening now?*

SE5: To see if it would happen the same way again. To some extent though, this has already been done, so it is unlikely to happen again.

ME: *What do you mean? Are you suggesting that you are not the first Source Entities to be created?*

Origin's Second Reinvention of Self

SE5: Correct. This is the second time the Origin has reinvented itself. The other Source Entities and I are the result of the second level of creation. We are not the first.

ME: *This is getting difficult for me to grasp now. I thought that the twelve current Source Entities were the first. I am sure that I understood this correctly. I am sure that my Source Entity, as well as the Origin itself, told about the moment when the Origin became self-aware and its decision to create the twelve Source Entities. The time (event) line seemed natural.*

SE5: That may be so, but the reality is that we are not the first.

ME: *So enlighten me. What did happen first?*

SE5: A prior experiment. The Origin simply duplicated itself. It copied itself a number of times.

ME: *I received the word "many times" then.*

SE5: The exact number is irrelevant. In that instance, the difference that it *duplicated* itself whereas what we have now is a *division* of self.

ME: *So where are the other Origins?*

This was an interesting turn of events as it corroborated an image I had a couple of years ago where I was sure I saw many Origins all huddled together. I had trouble understanding this and translated it into being the Source Entities altogether inside the Origin. Now it seems this image was one of a past event, one that was before the creation of the Source Entities.

Figure 1: Origins Huddled Together (4 versions)

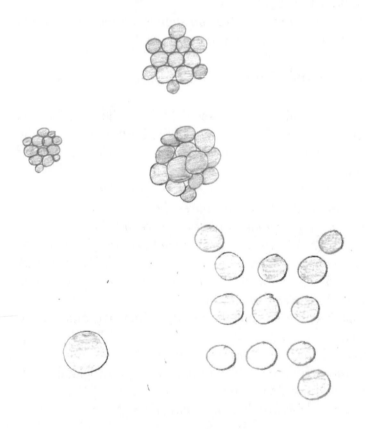

SE5:   It is highly possible that you saw this image when you were in communication with the Origin during your first reawakened excursions into your higher consciousness, for at that point you had not established any limits to work within.

ME: *How could you know that? This is the first time we have communicated, isn't it?*

SE5:   Yes, it is, but don't forget that I have all your knowledge, experience, and evolution in hand. As with the other Source Entities you have been in communication with, I was given a full history of your existence by your Source Entity before I embarked on this dialogue. We need this to help us understand what you can understand and how to communicate with you. Don't forget that it's hard for us to talk to you because of your limited vocabulary.

You are privileged to see such an image.

ME: *So I see.*

Thinking back, this image had given me cause for considerable concern. It was one that was potentially able to completely destroy the foundation of what little understanding I had of the Origin and the sequence of events surrounding its awakening and creation of the twelve Source Entities. It had me thinking along the lines that if there were more entities of the same quality as the Origin, there was something above the Origin that was big enough to contain them and be its own entity. What it didn't explain though was how the Origin could duplicate itself to a point where I could see an image of the duplicates from a distance. SE5 helped me with this conundrum.

SE5: The Origin exists within and without itself on all levels. It IS, always has been, and always will be the ALL. As such, to enable it to duplicate itself it created an environment within which it could be the dominant entity and then duplicated itself a dozen times, creating twelve equal entities.

ME: *Hold on. This seems a bit too much like the creation of the Source Entities.*

SE5: Of course. The Origin only changed the *process* of the strategy it was working on, not the direction it was going. The difference was that the Origin *duplicated* itself twelve times, not *divided* half of itself into twelve. This is a big difference in evolutionary thought for the Origin. The first work relied on each of those that were duplicated thinking that IT was ALL there was, instead of being one of twelve with THE Origin, of course, being the only one that knew of the others.

ME: *So why did the Origin change to its current strategy?*

SE5: Because the others either ran riot or extinguished themselves as a result of not accepting that they were the only one. It drove them quite mad.

ME: *But if THE Origin itself did not go mad or extinguish itself, why did the others?*

SE5: It had something to do with being the true first Origin, something to do with its properties. You will have to discuss this with the Origin yourself.

ME: *I intend to. I saw this as one of the chapters in a book I was planning, which I expect to title "The Origin Speaks."*

Wait a bit though, how could an Origin extinguish itself? I thought energy cannot be lost; it only changes form, so to speak.

SE5: It can't. What it does is dissolve its individuality, which means it gets re-absorbed into the Original Origin by default.

ME: *Let me get this straight. If an Origin that was created by the Origin could not dissolve itself or remove itself from individual existence, how does it get re-absorbed into the Original Origin?*

SE5: Because it is part of the natural make up of the Origin. I will explain further. The Origin IS the final frontier. It IS ALL THERE IS. There is NO-THING ELSE. So when the energy that is given sentience decides that it can no longer exist or no longer has the desire to exist for whatever reason, the association given to the energy of individuality and sentience is removed. The energy returns to Original Origin energy and essence. Let me give it to you in a simple format, albeit in a frequency-based example. If you reduce the frequency of the molecules of water to the point where the molecular movement is almost at a standstill (from your perspective), you also reduce its core temperature, creating ice. The ice will assume the form of the vessel that the water was being contained within and maintain it when it is decanted from it. If you consider that in the example given, the form the ice has assumed when its frequency is reduced is equal to the association of individuality and sentience to Origin energy. That association is only maintained whilst the frequency of the molecules is kept at the level necessary for water to become ice. Thus, you will understand that as the removal of the method used to reduce the frequency of the water to form ice results in the ice becoming water, a higher frequency energy. So does the removal of the association of Origin energy to give individuality and sentience make the energy return to that that it really is—Origin energy and essence.

ME: *Are you suggesting that the duplicated Origins are of a lower frequency to the Origin as a result of the Origin giving it individuality and sentience?*

SE5: It is not a matter of a different level of frequency; it's more a matter of a different level of "being" or "existence" of that energy.

Now that the Origin has its own recognition of self, it cannot remove that level of sentience or individuality from itself. It cannot destroy itself or remove the association of its own sentience from itself, for IT IS ALL THERE IS. However, when the association is removed, energy created from the Original Origin energy, whether duplicated or divided, will always return to what it was originally, Origin. Therefore, should the Origin remove the association to the Origin energy that it used to create the Source Entities, it would also return to the Origin as pure Origin energy essence.

ME: *This puts a whole new light on things for me. This means that everything we know could end in an instant should the Origin decide to change its strategy for experience and evolution. It could remove the association to individuality and sentience it has given to the energy used to create you and the other eleven Source Entities. I find that a bit scary!*

SE5: The thing you need to know is that this is not about to happen soon or even ever, according to my understanding.

ME: *Isn't that just wishful thinking?*

SE5: Not in the slightest. You see, the Source Entity strategy is so successful in terms of the experience and evolutionary opportunities that have been created and experienced that to stop it would be a backward step. There is simply too much momentum gained to warrant such a decision by the Origin. I will give you a classic example of why the Origin will never change its current strategy.

YOU are not alone.

ME: *What!?*

SE5: You are not alone. There are others like you experiencing existence at the lowest of frequencies that are able to penetrate the thin but almost impenetrable veil of the physical into the higher energetic realms. Some of you are even contacting the Origin directly as you are. This is a monumental experience for that part of you that is projected into the lower physical energies, your creator (your Source Entity), and the Origin. Never before has this happened. And what's more, it is happening in an area of your Source Entity that has been allowed to fall down the frequencies as far it could possibility go. And it is gathering pace.

Imagine the lowest of the low being in direct contact with the highest of the high. The lowest recognizing what it is communicating with and making interesting, intelligent, and constructive dialogue in the process while recognizing limitation but not being limited by its limitation. In the Origin's mind this is an unbelievable success. This is a level of continuity of expansion of awareness of self and the surrounding environment that is happening at all levels of entity. What's more, it appears to be both sustainable, and, expanding. Why would it destroy that, especially when there is more to come, much more from ALL of the Source Entities? The triangulation effect you have previously discussed with your own Source Entity not only applies to entities that are involved in existence in the physical frequencies associated with the entity you call Earth, it also applies across Source Entities as well.

ME: *Are you suggesting that we are in the throes of an evolutionary expansion of awareness that is, shall I say, unprecedented and unforeseen? Even by the Origin?*

SE5: Correct.

ME: *I am both shocked and surprised that the Origin could not foresee this happening. How could that be? With knowledge like this, I feel like I have come to the end of the book right here and now.*

SE5: You are not even at the start yet, believe me.

ME: *So what happens when this level of expansion in pan-Source consciousness finalizes? Will the Origin start again?*

SE5: Who knows? It has no plans.

I then gained an image of the Origin. It was full of the Source Entities and other smaller entities of similar stature. The only way I can describe this is that the Origin was smiling a benevolent smile. It was pleased with itself, its creations, and the creations that its creations had made. It was in company with like-minded individual entities of varying sizes and evolutionary status, all stemming from the original entities that were created by the Source Entities. Some had collated together to create a bigger entity of collective individuality Others had maintained their individuality. All were of single status. All had graduated from the need to be contained within the environments that their respective Source Entities had created for them. All were in direct communication with each other, the Source Entities, and the Origin itself. The Origin had created a community, a family, and it was well pleased.

ME: *What was that all about? Where did that image come from?*

SE5: That is the echo of what could be should the spark of conscious communication with the Source Entities and the Origin by those entities at its lowest levels of frequency continue. Remember that in your own communications with the Origin and your Source you were party to the fact that when the Origin was singular, it also lost contact with that part of itself that it projected into the lower frequencies.

ME: *I do remember that.*

SE5:   Well, this is an image of the Origin and all that has been created in its name that does not have the problem with losing contact with those parts of itself that reside in the lower frequencies, for they no longer exist.

Concurrent and Simultaneous Existence

ME: *That's fantastic. This tells me that at some time in the "future," the Origin and its creations will have evolved to the point where there are no lower frequencies where physical vehicles are needed to allow meaningful experience in different environments.*

SE5:   Correct. Not only that, but as I alluded to earlier, no one entity will be tied to the Source Entity that created it. They will all be free of the ties of their original environment. They will be equals with the Source Entities and the Origin, all within the Origin. In fact, in this particular event the Origin shifts its consciousness to be without itself rather than within as it currently is.

ME: *Hold on. You just said "in this particular event." That suggests to me that this is not a firm future—that it might not happen.*

SE5:   You humans are besotted with the use of time-based association for understanding the potential for concurrent and simultaneous existence. Everything that has, will, or could happen is happening right now.

ME: *Yes, I appreciate that, but it gives me the opinion that existence is still linear to a certain extent.*

SE5:   Only when you allow it to be. To a certain extent, it is true that the Origin and, indeed, ourselves, the Source Entities, became aware of self in a linear fashion. That is because that part of existence IS linear. But know this: once an entity is aware of its self and its environment, that level of existence diminishes. It ceases to be.

203

ME: *Why?*

SE5: Simply because the entity, in the process of realizing its self and its environment, realizes that everything that it does is mirrored in some way. When the entity in a now awakened state desires to know more about its environment and observes the events it created at a closer level of scrutiny, it notices that at every juncture where a major decision was made, the event is mirrored by a multiple equal to the number of options that could have been taken. The direction of those decisions all being played out to the next juncture where they can either stop or continue. The ability of an event to continue in a certain direction is based upon the energy behind the entity's desire to make that decision its real direction. For example, if an entity has a decision to make that has five different evolutionary opportunities and if two out of those five were desirable but only one was chosen, then the other three will carry on to the next juncture and stop whilst the other two will continue as if each of them had been the chosen direction.

ME: *So there aren't an infinite number of future possibilities?*

SE5: There are but the vast majority of them "run out of steam," as you say. Remember, energy needs to have thought-based intention to support it; otherwise, it has no role to play. Energy that has intention with it at all times is perpetuated to fruition and/or beyond. The myriad opportunities that are out there are the ones where there is enough intentional energy to support their continuation. As a result, the numbers of concurrent events that are occurring are self-governing. Let me elaborate a bit; every entity is surrounded by every possible move that it could make and what happens as a result of those moves. As the entity gains clarity of vision on what it wants to achieve and how it wants to achieve it, those events that correlate strongest with that vision stay with the entity. The others lose their association with the entity at the juncture where the correlation is weakest. The association is then broken but the event is recorded by the recording mechanism set up by the Source Entity for the environment that the entity exists within.

ME: *You speak as if you know that this is the functionality of concurrent existence in my Source Entities' environments.*

SE5: This is a common concept that exists across all Source Entities and their environments, and, before you ask, yes, it applies to Source Entities as well, irrespective of their creativity. In fact, it is also one that applies to the Origin. This is something that it discovered whilst in a state of its own singularity.

ME: *!?*

SE5: Yes, as you just pictured in your mind, this was understood by the Origin in the period before it created the Source Entities but after it duplicated itself.

ME: *That's interesting. I thought that the Origin was omnipotent and had no limitations.*

SE5: It doesn't. It is just a process that occurs as a result of an intention's longevity relative to its correlation with the underlying intention of an entity. Remove the intention to "be" from anything, and it will eventually flounder and return to the source of its creation. This is particularly true of discarded events. It is not true of discarded or ignored entities, for they continue to exist.

ME: *Can you tell me the difference between a concurrent event where a duplicate of the event has entities that surely must be created and an entity that is created for the purpose of existence and evolution? They must be the same, for aren't they both energy?*

SE5: An entity that is purposefully created for the task of experience and evolution is individualized and, therefore, autonomous to a certain extent, that extent being the prerogative of the creating entity. It will continue to exist even if ignored by the creating entity.

The mirrored entity that is created as a result of a strong intention to choose a certain event but that resulted in an equally strong intention to choose another event in its stead does not have individuality. It is an echo, a strong one though, that has the ability to continue in all of the possible directions it could go in should that direction have been chosen in preference to the one that was chosen. Should the original entity choose to go back to the event where the separation took place, however, and change direction to the discarded but nevertheless correlating direction, then that entity and direction gains individuality. The previous direction, now discarded, becomes the echo. It will retain its strong correlation with the original entity though until such time that the original entity changes back or correlation is no longer strong, at which point it will stop at the juncture where full separation is achieved.

ME: *Whilst you were describing that concept, I had an image of an almost wraith-like entity moving forward and being followed by other smaller transparent entities with some dropping out of sight while others are moving level with the entity. Once or twice I saw the one that moved up merge with the main entity, and it went in a different direction. It then twisted back and moved in a different direction. The smaller entity that merged now was made separate and dropped back a bit but still keeping pace with the original entity.*

Figure 2: The Wraith Entity

SE5: That is a good visualization. The movement of the entity is its movement through its own evolution, the others being the possible directions it could go should it make certain decisions. The opportunity to turn back and take a direction previously discarded was also seen illustrating the recognition of a wrong direction being taken. This will be a good concept to explain to your readers for it clears up the subject of concurrent/simultaneous existence nicely.

ME: *Don't worry. I will.*

In Closing

ME: *I do have to say that I am surprised to receive the information that the Origin is on its second experiment, we are part of the success of that second experiment, and the success could result in those entities being created by the Source Entities evolving beyond the need for association with their creators and being considered equals with them in the Origin's eyes.*

SE5: Why should you be surprised to gain confirmation on what you have witnessed and know is true?

ME: *I don't know. I just am.*

SE5: Let me tell you this while we are still communicating. The whole point of "your" existence in the earth sphere is to bring to the attention of mankind the fact that they exist within an energetic environment and have as long as they like to experience and evolve. The method for you to do this is to offer an alternative view to those authors that have gone before you. This means that you have been given the privilege of working directly with your Source, the remaining Sources, and the Origin in order to expand mankind's knowledge base into those areas that are of a quantifiable nature, namely the physics of the energetic and how to exist within it in an efficient way—one that does not allow an entity to get stuck within the frequencies where they are working. Better still, you are providing mankind information on the other Source Entities, such as me. Very soon mankind will be in a position to create machines that will prove spiritual texts, but it needs to have a framework to reference their findings. That reference is the texts created by spiritual authors who have experienced first-hand though meditation what scientists are just starting to detect on their machines.

My communication with you is to enable mankind to see that Source Entities are entities just like you, except we are created by the Origin directly. We are both bigger in energetic content and have unfathomable ability from your perspective. The environments and energetic inhabitants that populate those environments are a Source Entity's way of accelerating its evolution (evolution by devolution). Each has its own strategy on how it wants to achieve this task.

Each Source Entity is independent of the Origin to all intents and purposes even though it is part of the Origin and reports into the Origin.

In my existence I have decided to be singular and not create other environments (universes/multiverses), but I have decided to be more introspective via a "hands on" approach. To use the words of an actor, "I am my own stuntman. I use no doubles. What you perceive is what you get."

ME: *You must have created another entity at some point in your existence though? What about the thought entities you created by your first untrained thoughts.*

SE5: They were merely the creations of uncontrolled thoughts, thoughts with unrecognized intention.

In my existence I have considered the exploration of self a personal experience and task. It was not something that I wanted to experience via other creations, such as your Source Entity is experiencing through you. I wanted to experience that which is me as me.

ME: *Don't you feel alone? Especially when you know that the other Source Entities have created their own environments and sentient entities?*

SE5: Not in the slightest. You see, knowing that there are others like me that I am in communication with on a regular basis means that I am never alone. Don't forget that we are all in communion with the Origin as well. Furthermore, I actually enjoy the work that I do on my own. One of the things that I find particularly interesting is the slow but steady increase in smaller entities created by my peers discovering existence outside of their own environments and initiating dialogue. This is the start of the evolutionary change that you saw in your vision. What's more, some of these entities are starting to communicate across Source Entity environmental boundaries. You will experience this in the communications associated with the next book you will be compiling.

ME: *I thought Earth was a pivotal point in my universe?*

SE5: It is one of the specific areas in your Sources' environments where this is taking place, and it is happening in similar areas in other Source Entity environments. However, it has a very, very long way to go before it gets anywhere near the image you saw.

ME: *As a said before, with this level of information coming out, I sort of wonder if I need to carry on in this direction rather than continuing my dialogues with the remaining Source Entities.*

SE5: Our dialogue with you is an important milestone in mankind's increase in spiritual knowledge. As a result, you must continue along this path for it will help in making the picture clearer. Without a firm foundation in basic knowledge, higher knowledge is meaningless for the gap is too big to jump successfully

ME: *Yes, I understand.*

SE5: I believe you do.

Before I leave you, so you can continue your journey of dialogue, I will fill in a gap for you relating to my existence. I am aware that I have been sparse in my explanation.

ME: *What is it that you want to advise me of?*

SE5: As a singular entity experiencing and evolving in the singular, I also contribute in a significant way to the Origin's evolution. This is because many of the Sources have created other entities and not remained singular. As a result, the opportunity presented to me to experience and experiment as a single entity was compelling. In its desire to have its creations create, this was an area of evolution that could have been missed by the Origin. Based upon this, my singularity is an important undertaking. I am as it were, filling in an important gap, one that was almost missed.

ME: *How could the Origin miss such an opportunity? I would not expect the master of all, the omnipresent creator to miss anything.*

SE5: That singular conundrum is one of the reasons why the Origin created us—to fill in the gaps. It realized very quickly that it was so vast and its desire to evolve was so strong that it would need to get help or miss a trick or two. You have received this information in past dialogues, have you not?

ME: *Yes, I believe I have.*

SE5: Then it should not be a surprise to learn that even the Origin has a level of fallibility, and the route that it has taken to evolve is the fastest possible route available to alleviate this fallibility. Evolution is a wonderful tool, for with evolution comes wisdom and understanding, which, in turn, negate fallibility. My creation and my acceptance to remain singular have allowed the Origin to evolve, gain further wisdom, and reduce its fallibility. Hence, it is an honor for me to remain singular. These are the reasons why I remained singular.

Go now and contemplate this information, for you have the other Sources to talk to.

As the link was removed from Source Entity Five, I gained the impression that I could have obtained much more detail of its experiments. Although the information passed on to me was not specifically about SE5 itself, it was new, fresh, and to my knowledge unknown by man. As a result, the dialogue was a success, and I was grateful for SE5 allowing me to link into it.

As I sat in contemplation, my thoughts went back to an image I received about the communication between entities from different Source Entities. It was presented to me as a crisscross of lines between entities within entities within entities. It felt wonderful to have been shown this "progressive" change and development towards total independence of our Source Entities. I knew I would discuss this again later when I am gathering the dialogues for Source Entities Seven to Twelve as Source Entity Five had suggested that I would. I was full of excitement. I then looked forward to my next Source Entity, Source Entity Six. The image I received was that of a huge five-pointed star. What did that mean?

Chapter 6:

Source Entity Six

Initial Contact with SE6

It had been over a week since I had finished my dialogue with
Source Entity Five, and it was some three months since I had
communicated with my own Source Entity. Although I was
aware that it was with me at all times, it is good to touch base
once in a while. It took seconds to access the correct level to
initiate communication.

SE: I see that you are doing well with my counterparts.

ME: *It's amazing how easy the conversations are going so
far. I am also constantly surprised at the information
that is being given to me. I seem to get more diverse
information when I think that I can't possibly receive
anything else, but that is my issue, especially when I
start to try to rationalize the information, as my limited
Earth-based knowledge gets in the way.*

SE: Correct. It is always best to just receive and not
intellectualize what is being given to you. My
counterparts have worked hard to make your
communication experience as easy as possible. The last
Source Entity, whom you called Source Entity Five,
emulated my frequency to the point where it was almost
indistinguishable from mine. That made it much easier
for you.

ME: *Ah! That would explain the feeling I had that the
conversation was so "matter of fact" that I had a doubt
in the back of my mind that I was actually
communicating with Source Entity Five—that in fact, I*

was communicating with you. I found that most disturbing, to say the least, for I feared that the content would be invalid.

SE: Source Entity Five's ability to simulate my frequencies is a product of the shared learning that we all experience. As you have been advised previously, we share our learning with each other and the Origin just as you share your knowledge with me. That is the deal. As a result, the methods of how to communicate with you get passed on to each new Source Entity you talk to. Hence, they start with a better "interface" than they would have if they had started from scratch. Each Source Entity then improves the link and makes the improvement available to all. At this point then, the link is about as good as it will get with your limited "band width."

ME: So I can't expect much more improvement then?

SE: No, not in your current condition. However, you will be much, much better when you are disincarnate.

ME: I look forward to that.

SE: I see that you do.

ME: Why did I get an image of a five-pointed star to represent Source Entity Six at the end of the last chapter?

SE: Why don't you ask Source Entity Six yourself? It is waiting for you to start a dialogue.

ME: O.K., O.K., I get the hint. It's time to move on, I take it.

SE: It is. Time is not of the essence though.

ME: ?! I will question you on that comment later.

SE: No, now is best. Don't rush your desire to finish. Communication with this Source will be easier then.

Five Aspects—Five Levels of Existence

ME: I can see the shape of a five-pointed star in my mind's

eye again. Source Entity Six, can I refer to you as such?
SE6: You may.
ME: Why do I see you in this imagery?
SE6: The five-pointed star represents the five aspects of me. Each aspect is a level of existence.
ME: Whoa! At this point I was thinking of asking you about your early existence and how you became sentient, etc.
SE6: That is not necessary, for it would be a similar story to the other Source Entities that you have and will communicate with.
ME: O.K., Point taken. I guess one of the reasons we are communicating so fluently is because of the learning you have gained from my other dialogues.
SE6: Correct. I would not say that the Source Entities were all lined up in a queue to talk to you, but we have been following with interest and learning as a result.
ME: Tell me about your five levels of existence then.
SE6: Let me explain the reasons for their existence first.

Whereas your Source has dimensions—each with a frequency component and each leading to a path that is closer to itself—I have levels of existence with no dimensions and no frequencies. Of course, dimension and frequency are fundamental parts of my make-up, but I have not used them as tools to divide those parts of me that are used as levels of existence. If you want to use such nomenclature, then that is O.K., so long as you consider it to be five *composite* dimensions with a *single* base frequency in each dimension.
ME: What do you mean by the term "composite dimension"?
SE6: Consider it in this way. Sorry, can I access your mind at will to find the correct words to describe this concept?
ME: Be my guest.
SE6: Mmm, O.K. The best way I can describe it is by using your video transmission technology by wire. Consider that your base dimension is actually three dimensions

linked together to create one liveable environment, and the upper dimensions add onto these dimensions to create the next environment. At a certain point upwards in the dimensional structure, all you need is one dimension to exist within as the lower dimensions added together create the bare minimum dimensional requirement for the existence of sentient energetic life. So you have three dimensions equal one dimensional level, four dimensions equal the next dimensional level—the true second level—five dimensions equals the true third level, and so on. The need for the three base dimensions is not required past the fourth. The first three are separate but necessarily together to create the first true dimension. In my creation, I don't need the first three, which would be like the separate RGB (red, green, blue) wires/channels you have in some of your basic video hardware. The fourth, audio, represents the next (second true) dimension and is a separate wire as well. I have the equivalent of composite RGB and audio—which is a single wire system with three video signals, red, green, and blue, and audio (representing the fourth dimension in your multiverse)—all being transmitted over the wire at the same time. Henceforth, a composite RGB audio system represents the structure in a simple way for each of my levels of existence—each being self-contained and independent of each other. Each is a level of existence that my sentient creations must experience in full.

ME: *That's a good simple explanation. Thank you. So what does each of the levels represent?*

SE6: They are as follows:

- Level 1 is the level of basic existence and understanding of self and sentience
- Level 2 is the level of self-realization, awareness of my greater reality

- Level 3 is the level of creativity
- Level4 is the recognition of creativity for evolutionary purposes
- Level 5 is the level of evolutionary experience through self-denial, the ultimate sacrifice

ME: *Can you explain how your creations experience each of the levels?*

SE6: Of course, but before we start with the first level, I want to advise you that my creations don't need to experience these levels in order, for they are not a progression towards myself like you have with your Source. Each entity can become part of me or separate from me at any time.

ME: *Do any of your creations experience existence in the same levels of physicality as we do here on earth?*

SE6: No, not in a way that you would understand. Hang on to that question though, as I will answer it in full later.

ME: *Hang on a moment. I have just realized that the explanation of the levels do, in fact, suggest progression of some sort. How can this be? It doesn't make sense.*

SE6: That is because you are thinking in a linear fashion. That is a product of your current existence. My creations are given the ability to limit their knowledge, wisdom, and ability relative to the level they are working in for the duration of their existence. To do this, they are created with a level of experience and knowledge that is enough to allow them to operate in any of the levels either singularly or concurrently. Most of them work on more than one level concurrently, and they need not be levels that are adjacent each other.

ME: *I am starting to get confused. How can they work on different levels at the same time?*

SE6: By duplicating themselves. This is a fundamental ability that all my creations have. They can duplicate themselves in a number of different ways; each way can also be tailored to the creation's specific experience requirements in order for them to get the most out of their existence.

ME: *I know that this is going to sound a bit weak, but what do they experience in Level 1, for example?*

SE6: In Level 1 they have to exist in groups with a purpose. Each group has a basic role to play in its existence. That role may be to create a great civilization or simply what you would call a village. The task at hand is for them to enter into this group with a high level of single-minded determination, so much determination, in fact, that they are fully engrossed in their environment to the point where they are not aware of what or who they are. The task then is to break out of this mold and realize that they are more than they are or what they experience.

ME: *From what I can see here, they are their own experiment in awareness.*

SE6: That's correct. The awareness part is the first step on the ladder to recognizing sentience.

ME: *What have they created in the past to achieve such recognition of self?*

SE6: Some of them have explored their environment in ways that are similar to your mankind's exploration of Earth. Others have taken a more introspective position and used a form of meditation to achieve it.

ME: *Can you give me an example of the exploration side of things? For instance, what are they exploring?*

SE6: They group together to form a bigger creation (entity). This gives them an increase of collective ability. That allows them to explore their current level in a mental aspect rather than in what you would call machines. In doing this, they start to learn the meaning of self through singularity versus collectivity and what they can achieve with these conditions. Therefore, recognition of sentience is a byproduct of this because when they realize there are differing outputs and levels of success in what is experienced or found during exploration into differing levels of collectivity, they begin to experiment. A fundamental component of being able to plan and experiment is the ability to learn, plan, discuss, and review, and this requires sentience.

ME: *This sounds like a very similar evolutionary route to that described by Source Entity Four where the entities grouped together to create what I called "cities."*

SE6: It is similar, but they are on a smaller scale. The entities that I have created can and do anything they want to achieve their goals. In the first level of existence, the environmental aspect is much the same as a physical environment with the exception that the entities can blend and merge with the materials that make up the physicality of the Level 1 environment. They exist in areas of plane physical energy.

ME: *What is "plane physical energy"? This is a term I have not come across before.*

SE6: Plane physical energy is energy that is essentially two-dimensional.

ME: *You mean it is flat.*

SE6: Not is the way that you are thinking. An energy plane is an area of energy that is frequentially flat. That means that there are no high or low spots in the frequencies that make it up. In one of your discussions with your own Source Entity, the ability to move upwards or downwards through the frequencies was described by using those areas of high and low frequency that are close to each other, the low portion of a higher frequency being located near a high portion of a low frequency. This is not possible in a physical plane energy environment, for the entities are not able to affect the energies in a positive or negative fashion.

Description of One of SE6's Entities

ME: *I am having trouble getting my head around this one. I am receiving an image of an area that looks like a very flat area of cloud-like material with what look like fish jumping in and out of the upper and lower layer of the cloud. They never escape the cloud though.*

SE6: That is a very filtered image you are receiving. I will try to clarify it a bit for you.

With this new image, I saw that the fish were actually dark multi-layered entities. Streamers of dark energy emanated from them as they moved. I zoomed in to the image of the entity to get a better "look." It was like an amorphous black hole. The interior, which was visible, was the exterior, which was the interior; everything was confused as if it was all one and the same. From the outside it looked like the inside was full of star-like objects, objects that moved in procession, each having a direction to go. Everything about the entity defied the physical logic of what I was used to. Indeed, it was multi-layered and possibly multi-dimensional whilst existing within a Level 1 environment that was supposed to be two-dimensional. I was starting to realize that the two-dimensionality that I was used to was not what was being explained here. I decided to continue with the information that I was getting from the image of the entity I was linked to and discuss this matter of the dimensionality of a multi-dimensional being in a two-dimensional effect of plane physical energy later. I re-focused my mind's eye.

The entity seemed to be interconnected in all ways possible—the inside was the outside, the middle was the end, and the center was the periphery. In all this though, there was an element of order. Everything had a function. As I looked into the heart of the entity, I saw what I can only describe as organs—areas of similar energy that were standing alone, appearing to have a job to do. Looking further, the images of stars that I received in my first glance at the entity were rewarded with more definition. The stars were pockets of energy of differing quantity, quality, and functional importance to the continuing existence of the entity.

So that is what Source Entity Six meant when he said that these entities were physical. They needed energy of sorts, working with parts of themselves to make their existence possible. Although Source Entity Six created them, they needed to work with the energies of the five levels of existence to allow their continuation. As I started to understand this, I noticed that certain parts of the entity were not working with the "star" energies. They were immobile. These parts I conjectured, were those "organs" that were necessary to allow the entity to exist within the other levels of existence. Then suddenly, it all fell into place. The image of the entity was not of an entity that was constrained to working with one level of existence; it was working with two levels of existence concurrently. The "inside-outness" was a result of being connected to the two levels/environments, or was it? I decided to confirm this thought process with Source Entity Six.

SE6: The entity you logged into is, in fact, working with more than one level of existence, but its appearance is not a result of its duality. The organs, as you call them, are multifunctional in terms of their ability to work in the five different environments. As a result, some of them are not needed and so are not used. There are times when all of the organs are used and others when none are used. Logically speaking, the organs are used to their maximum potential when an entity is existing in all five levels at the same time. They are redundant when the entity is in existence outside of the five levels of existence.

ME: *When would the entity not be within the five levels of*

221

existence? When they have finished their evolutionary tasks?

SE6: No. They, like you, need to review what they have been experiencing and what the benefit to themselves and me such experiences have given them. What you have witnessed in the entity you have logged into is the appearance of that entity to me or an outside observer. That part of the entity that is in the level of existence is not aware of the additional parts of itself that are in existence, so it is not able to manipulate those parts of its selves that are in other levels. What I will say is that the entities are aware of those parts of themselves that are focused upon the various levels of existence available when they are external to the levels. I will elaborate further. What you saw was, indeed, a multi-dimensional entity existing within a two-dimensional level of plane physical energy. The description of the entity that I have just given you refers to a higher level of dimensionality, which you have not yet perceived.

ME: *Now I am confused. What do you mean by a higher level of dimensionality than I have been used to/perceived?*

SE6: In your existence you have only experienced and considered multi-dimensional existence in terms of the ability to move within and between the dimensions that you are associated with. Even when you are in multi-dimensional existence, you are singular in application. You separate yourself out—one portion of yourself for each dimensional environment. You even do this for the frequencies in between the dimensions. This is a function of your energetic species, not of your "self." In my environments the physical entity is truly able to exist in all dimensions simultaneously—hence, the aspect of the image that you received. You would be advised to link into it (the entity) again to gain further knowledge of its construction.

ME: *Does the entity mind that I am critiquing it?*

SE6: It is not aware of your signature and so will not detect you openly.

I focused my attention on the entity in question. It suddenly struck me how bizarre this may seem to the uninitiated amongst us. That I am in communication with an entity and its creator, with its potential physical distance being what our scientists would consider to be sextillions upon sextillions upon sextillions of parsecs away from our Earthly location. If I hadn't known deep down that this was normal in the energetic, I would have considered it pure fiction, a daydream, perhaps even psychotic delusion. The image that appeared in my mind reminded me that even a deluded mind could not think up such images and explanations to unknown questions, questions and answers that could be explained in hard physics, even if it is physics that humankind has not yet been exposed to, except via spiritual physicists. Considering that the greater reality is so rich in stimulus, it was not hard for me to understand how humankind projected into the physicality of the Earth sphere is considered to be in a very, very deep dream state, a state of extreme sense deprivation. I focused on the task at hand and tried to see if I could gain more information on this entity.

Upon closer examination, it appeared that the entity was constructed in an energetic way that was consistent with its environmental needs. Aren't we all, I thought! But I looked further and closer. Further in terms of the detail of its interface with the dimensions, moving into and out of all the dimensions associated with the entity, and closer in terms of the application of the detail, how it worked energetically.

As a whole entity, it was linked with every environmental consideration that Source Entity Six had created, which was very, very complicated, to say the least. I had been looking at this entity as an outsider from the same perspective as its

Source Entity and, as a result, seen it in its entirety. As I modified my focus to the levels of the entity that were associated with each of the composite dimensions aligned to the levels of existence, I noticed that the other parts of the entity, those not aligned, tuned out (became invisible). This gave a rather strange appearance to the entity. Parts of its "body" were not physically or energetically connected but were clearly still associated with it. To use a human description of this condition, it was rather like the torso of a body moving around without any legs or one of its arms connected but with those limbs and the functions associated to those limbs still working as though connected to the torso.

The entity being observed, of course, looked nothing like a human being, but it did have form, albeit randomised because of its current condition, waif-like. In this current condition, the relationship between what I would call an exterior and an interior was still upside down and inside out, so to speak, but it had a discernable purpose. With the filter of just seeing one of the levels that the entity was working with firmly in place, I could see that there was a sort of lose Möbius loop effect in place. Not in the sense of the popular set of stairs that you climb up even though you are going down example but more in terms of how the energies worked within the entity. The "star" shaped pockets of energy would still move in procession into and out of certain areas of stable energy that I had previously suggested may be organs of some type, but I couldn't actually be sure that it was the same energy that entered the "organ being observed" was the same coming out.

I decided to take an even closer look.

No, I was right to question what I was seeing. One type of energy was going into one side of the "organ," and a different type of energy was coming out. I changed the focus of my mind's eye to the other level the entity was working on and noted that where there was a void in between the organs of the entity in the previous level, there was now a functioning part of the body of the entity that was working with the energies that had, I now know, gone into one side of the organ and disappeared, only to be replaced with an energy of a different type that exited the organ that had been processed by an organ present on the other level. The organs and parts of the entity's body that were in the first level had now disappeared. They were still there, but they were on the first level.

Again it started to fall into place. The organs weren't organs at all. They were portals, mini-doorways within the entity that not only allowed the energies and those parts of its form to exist on the different levels they were, but allowed both the energy flow between those parts and the interactive functionality of the entity's form on one level to also function in between levels concurrently with the other level. I was being shown how an entity of supposed physicality, plane physical energy, cannot only exist in different levels but is designed to function in these levels at the same time. As a result of this function, its form was not really form but pure function. The forms that I could see, I now noted, would change, albeit subtly, to the demands of the function of the entity within the level that it was working on and the experience it was having. I was just thinking that I couldn't possibly describe the physicality of the entity being observed when Source Entity Six came to my rescue.

SE6: The entity you have observed cannot be fully explained in any form of detail with the language you are using to chronicle this dialogue. What you have described though is a reasonable attempt to give a vague overview. For this you should be applauded. One piece of additional information I will give you about this entity is that its dimensions (size), if you want to call them that, are equal to the size of one of your universes. You may want to consider them as a universal entity rather than an entity of similar stature to yourself.

Now I was in a different league, I thought. An entity that was existing in its normal everyday way in more than one environment/level at once, whose essence was twisted and turned to suit the demands of those environments whilst staying connected, and the size of which was on the universal scale compared to my physical level of understanding, was, to be perfectly honest, mind blowing!!

I never gave a thought to the possibility of scale here. How many other entities had I seen in my mind's eye that I thought were similar in size at least to my own energetic self but were either on the universal scale, the micro-universal scale, the atomic in physical terms, or even the macro-universal scale? I very quickly came to the conclusion that to dwell on such a conundrum would not benefit the work that I was doing. It would only serve to confuse my perspective and lose confidence in my ability. What does scale matter in the greater scheme of things where experience and evolution are the main reason for existence? Momentarily, I contacted the entity I was observing, not in terms of communication but in terms of observation. I received, though, a message from the entity to look deeper into its function, how it worked and existed. It advised me that it was one of a vast number of entities, that the area it occupied was infinitesimal compared to the totality of Source Entity Six and that it was not the singular item that I thought it was even though in essence, it was. Confused, this prompted me to take its advice of looking deeper into the entity.

I received what I thought was conflicting information, but upon reflection it made total sense within the scheme of Source Entity Six's creativity. The stars that appeared to part the flow of energy between the "organs," the gateways between those parts of the entity that were in the different levels, what I called energy, were not what they seemed. As I recalibrated my attention, I noticed that they were not just energy but were structured energy, energy with purpose. I needed a better look at this, so I again recalibrated my mental vision. The stars were smaller universal entities, ones within a greater universal entity with the smaller universal entities being part of the essential function of the large universal entity. This wasn't the reason for my initial thoughts on contradiction though; there was a more convoluted game afoot here.

I had noticed that there was a strong image in my mind relating the smaller universal entities to the larger universal entities— one that I couldn't shake. With it came the knowledge assigned to the image. It was slow at first, but as I started to accept and understand, the information came stronger and faster. The smaller universal entities were, in fact, the larger universal entities—the scale of which had been adjusted to allow the involvement within the confines of their peers. As I was typing this text, I was corrected. It was not the scale of the entity that was changed to allow them to work within what I described as the larger universal entity (a large universal entity within a large universal entity) but the perspective. I understood perspective to be a method that artists used to give a limited 3D effect in their painting/drawings; it was also used a lot in architectural drawings especially those used to give the "artist's impression" of new buildings, malls, or complexes. How could a change in perspective allow the appearance of scale to be changed to such a huge difference? I really needed to ask Source Entity Six about this as it was really starting to confuse me. Imagine the implications of entities on a universal scale that were not only able to work and exist within different levels, dimensions, and frequencies, but were also able to work within and without each other whilst being in this multi-level/dimensional perspective state. The word DIFFICULT!!! rang in my ears. Source Entity Six came to my rescue.

Figure 1: Source Entity Six's Entities

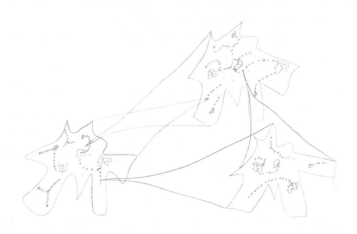

SE6: Perspective is the only word that I/you could use that would give you the understanding you need here. I will describe it in a different way. I can see that you are already receiving the supporting imagery.

ME: *Yes, I just received the image of a telescope, zooming out to see the image of what I will now call the "outside" large universal entity and then zooming in to see what I will call the "inside" large universal entity. However, I also know that the "inside" large universal entity also has universal entities associated with it "inside" its perspective and that the larger universal entity is similarly associated with another universal entity in "inside" perspective. Phew, this is all very interrelated.*

SE6: Visually that is a good description but energetically it behaves in an altogether different way. Using the perspective analogy, I will explain further. If YOU were the "inside" entity looking out at the "outside" entity, it would look like it was "inside" you.

ME: *Are you suggesting that there is a distance component to this description?*

SE6: No, it is not distance. It is an effect of the perspective.

ME: *But to me that is distance. This is bending my mind like a dimensional pretzel!*

SE6: What a good image to use. The pretzel, in some versions, can be considered as a Möbius loop. The effect that you are experiencing/seeing is based upon the interaction of entities when they are nominally based in different levels and locations within the dimensions. Remember that the dimensions in these levels are composite and so are not reliant on the factor of three that you experience in your own environment. In effect the dimensions are blurred together so that there is no demarcation between them. As a result of this "blurring" of the "edges," an entity can be within and without a, let me say, "dimension within the composite dimension" I will call it a "cimension," concurrently. The interaction between the entities is such that the cimensions within each of the levels are similarly blurred and relative to the area (volume) of the level and corresponding composite dimension associated with the level of existence being experienced. Everything and every entity is linked in every way as a result, and every entity is reliant on each other for its continued functionality, for they all form the essence of each other on every level.

ME: *So how do they achieve singular experience and evolution if they are interconnected in such a way?*

SE6: They achieve singular experience due to the focus of intention by that part of the entity that is designed to assign the experience to the "packet" of energy that can be identified as a specific entity with known signature and direction.

ME: *So individuality is based upon a collective set of energies working together in a collectively agreed way and purpose.*

SE6: Yes, but don't forget that because they are all interconnected and related, they are all working on each other's purpose as well.

Just when I was starting to understand a little!

Basic Functions of the Five Levels Created by SE6

As usual with my work, I had noticed that I had moved away from my agenda of understanding certain principles surrounding the environment that a Source Entity, in this instance, Source Entity Six, had created in its effort to experience, learn, and evolve. The interlude that described in summary the entity's form or lack of it and the interconnectedness between the entities and their environment had been fascinating, if not mind bending to say the least. The images received were of a most interesting quality. I made a mental note to myself to try to draw what I had seen. I was keen though to press on and gain a greater level of detail than already received on the workings behind the five levels. I decided to tackle each one in order, taking into account that the entities themselves can work in more than one level concurrently and that they can be part of each other in a most integral way dimensionally and functionally. I had a feeling that the "one liners" were nowhere near descriptive enough to allow an understanding of their real meaning.

ME: *In a previous dialogue with you, I was given the basic functions in one line for the levels that you created. I would like to expand on these levels and their functions/opportunities for evolution.*

SE6: We can discuss this if you like. I warn you though, the descriptions will be basic—just enough for you to understand and convey to your "readers" their function. Where possible I might introduce the physics of them

ME: *That's fine.*

Level 1—Basic Existence, Understanding Self, Gaining Sentience

ME: *You described the first level as the level of basic existence and understanding of self and sentience. Can you elaborate on what this level means from an environmental perspective?*

SE6: Remember that each level has its own composite dimension to inflate it and allow its existence and usability, and when an entity has reached a certain level of evolutionary growth, it can re-enter this environment concurrently with the existence within other levels. It does this with a view to experience the wonder of experiencing the "first" awakening process again with the possibility of maybe changing the way it reacted to see if it could have evolved faster as a result.

ME: *Yes, I do remember.*

SE6: Good. Then note that each of the levels has an energetic functionality that is consistent with the objectives of the environmental level being experienced. In the case of the first level, the energetic functionality is rather basic. In this level the entity is considered to be in the first stage of awakening from being raw energy to being energy with sentience. The first level environment has what you would call a "child lock" function on the entity's ability to command and create from the surrounding energies it finds itself in. In essence all that the entity can do is exist and experience its "self" and the others that are also within this level.

The energies in this level are subtle and supportive of the newly awakened entity, providing it with all its basic needs.

ME: *What needs would those be?*

SE6: At this point the entity is not self-supporting in the generation of its own energies—those needed to continue its own existence.

ME: *It needs food?*

SE6: In a figure of speech, yes, but not food in the sense that you are considering. Let us consider one of the most sentient beings on your planet as an example, the dolphin in its physical state. As a mammal, when the dolphin is first born, it needs to breathe. This is the most critical part of its short existence in separation from its mother. The female dolphins assist the newborn to the surface of the sea to help it take its first breath. In the time taken to move/be moved from its location of birth to the surface, it learns the fundamentals of controlling its physical body and the rudimentary method of communication used by the females that surround it.

ME: *It's that fast?*

SE6: It's that fast. It's a similar process for the newly awakened energies that form the entity in the first level with the exception that it does not need to rise to the surface, and it does not need to breathe air. It does, however, need to be able to use the energies around it, integrate them into its own volume, and further integrate itself into the energies that exist within the composite dimension that is Level 1.

ME: *I have a sudden feeling that they have to do this because if they don't, they get rejected by the energies that make up Level 1. Why would I be receiving this sort of information? I find it strange that the energies in the level would reject an entity that it is designed to support.*

SE6: It is not in the slightest bit strange. The need to be part of the level they are working with is a fundamental function that they have to do in all aspects of their existence. It is the equivalent of the dolphin's need to learn to breathe air and communicate with its female helpers. In this instance, the entity is learning, understanding, and applying the basis for its existence and evolution—integration. It is an important lesson that needs to be learned and understood from the very onset of awakening, for it sustains its very being. You will notice from the previous dialogue that the entities work with and integrate with several levels at the same time, including with each other in a major/macro and minor/micro sense. So the need to integrate with the energies of the level that they find themselves upon awakening is an immediate and urgent requirement. Failure to do so within a specific period results in the energies of the level rejecting the entity as a non-entity, a virus if you like. The speed of integration with the energies of the environment determines the potential speed of evolution of an entity. If you like, it determines how steep the evolution curve is going to be. The steeper the curve, the faster the evolution, and the shorter the time for re-integration with me. This is similar in your Source Entity's environment, for the highly evolved entities can and do have the opportunity to become one with their Source.

ME: *So the basis of basic existence in this example is the full and complete integration of the entity with the energies of the environment they are within.*

SE6: Correct.

ME: *Sounds like it's a very short lesson.*

SE6: It doesn't finish there.

ME: *Ah, I didn't see that coming.*

SE6: Oh yes, you did.

ME: *You got me.*

SE6: Once integrated into the environmental energies of the level, they have to prove that they are in control of those energies. They must learn to define the difference between the environmental energies that are part of them and those that are part of the environment, including those that are integrated and de-integrated in a transient fashion. This is the road to the true understanding of self which is a pre-requisite to sentience.

ME: *So it's like a very basic environment where the entity is allowed to develop its most basic autonomous and mental faculties, so to speak.*

SE6: Correct. The innate knowledge about the need to integrate—you might call it instinct—is accelerated by the even more innate knowledge that lack of integration results in rejection. Level 1 is, therefore, like being in kindergarten (nursery school) where an entity learns, experiences, and evolves on the most basic levels. Recognition of this by the entity is the key to sentience.

Level 2—Self-Realization

ME: *You described Level 2 as the level of self-realization and awareness of your greater reality. Can you elaborate further because in my mind this is very similar to Level 1's evolutionary opportunities?*

SE6: It appears to be similar, but in actuality it is not. If you were to look at the basic descriptions of Level 1 and Level 2, you should notice a familiar similarity with your own environment. Level 1 is where most of humankind is currently, and Level 2 is where some of you are evolving toward or are currently evolved at. Your current "incarnate" state classifies as being within Level 2, but energetically you are much further. Full self-realization and full awareness via constant experience would put an entity in your environment at the end of Level 2's evolutionary opportunities, with entities at this level knocking on the door of level 3 if you were following them in sequence, that is.

ME: *That's a good comparison, thank you. How does that translate into what you expect your entities to be experiencing?*

SE6: The answer to that question is as simple as your own, but I will elaborate because as you have experienced in one of our previous dialogues, my entities cannot in reality be compared to your humankind.

ME: *Please carry on.*

SE6: Self-realization for my entities is a significant step on the evolutionary ladder. Once they have progressed from Level 1 to Level 2, they are considered to be autonomous units of energy, working together with other entities and those energies they find themselves existing within. Self-realization is the absolute knowledge and constant understanding on a very deep down, personal experiential level. It is not a theory or a discussion between entities or even a belief system. It is a working everyday experience where the entity knows and works with the experiences it is having that are outside its normal level of understanding, which would be recognition of self and its environment and contemporaries. A self-realized entity recognizes that it is part of something much bigger than it is currently aware of to the point that its individual experience is enhanced to encompass the greater reality that it was either previously not aware of or chose to ignore for some reason. With my entities, that level of self-realization is the understanding and experiential experience of the way they can be part of other entities in a micro-universal sense or have other entities existing with and within them as part of their micro-universal condition—themselves being the macro-universal entities. Continued development of self-realization results in the entities recognizing that there is a link between some of the entities they are working with and a greater reality. That greater reality at first is the recognition that these "interfacing" entities don't exist in their entirety within the environment supported by the level they are currently working within. Indeed, they are only within the level that they first recognized as the environment that they were existing within in a reduced sense—that is, there is more to the entity, and that it is somewhere else: in another level.

Know this:

There is a vast difference in the evolutionary level of an entity that intellectually recognizes the "fact" that there are different levels of existence and different ways of which it as an autonomous entity can be integrated with other entities and one where the entity knows both intellectually and experientially that these levels exist. In fact, they exist in an integrated, autonomous way with their fellow entities and can work and manipulate the energies that are either part of the entity or level that they are part of to enhance their own experience quotient and evolution.

This is the difference between the novice and the master, the chela and the guru. When the chela has reached the master stage and the guru is close to or is a mahavatar, it is time for the mahavatar to be elevated to the next level to be a chela again—albeit one of a much evolved level but nevertheless a beginner at the new level it has ascended to, which in this instance would be Level 3.

ME: *My understanding is that an entity that was considered to be a mahavatar was one that was in constant communion with Christ and his/its energies.*

SE6: That is an analogy that works well in your plane of

existence. In my environments I would suggest that the mahavatar is an entity that is both aware of the master/guru level and is in frequent or constant dialogue with me (mahavatar level) while on the verge of "universal" creativity. The level of creativity of the mahavatar in your environment is limited to localized creativity, on what you would call the planetary scale. When my entities reach this level of attainment, they are capable of creating vast macro/micro-universes of their own that are interspersed with those universes that are both created by their counterparts and are part of or the whole of themselves. They do this because they are from your perspective universal in nature, volume, and ability. Your own universe created by your Source Entity is an entity in its own right and has its own evolution to consider when working with the smaller entities, such as yourself.

ME: *Yes. I am aware of that. The Source Entity of my multiverse discussed this with me in one of my previous dialogues in* The History of God: a story of the beginning of everything. *We even discussed the hierarchy of the universe, galaxy, solar system, and planetary systems as a physical and energetic function of its creation.*

SE6: Good, then note that the entities in my environment do not create such hierarchies per se as they each perform that role themselves within and without each other's boundaries. As we discussed before, they are universal in nature and in creation.

I felt that we had exhausted the dialogue on this particular level, and, as a result, decided that it was time to move on to Level 3. Although, in the back of my mind I did feel that in this particular instance of self-realization and awareness, it was uncannily close to the description that a number of notable spiritual movements use. Maybe it was universal? I decided to ask this one last question whilst in the discussion about Level 2 and its functions in the evolutionary toolbox.

ME: *This all sounds too familiar to me. It's as if it is a standard or a constant.*

SE6: Well perceived. Just as the need to evolve is a constant desire within the framework of all the Origin's creations, so is the need to be in an initial position of so-called ignorance. Striving to be self-aware of position and relationship with the absolute and the creator, the Origin, is a necessary and fundamental route to accelerated evolution. This is why your Source Entity created your physical universe in the frequencies and dimensions it is—in order to experiment in accelerated evolution through the realization of self as a progression from ignorance in the harshest possible environment.

Level 3—Creativity

ME: *As you previously mentioned, Level 3 is the level of creativity. This sounds like a very important level to me as creativity is one of the precursors to evolution.*

SE6: Correct. To be creative is quite possibly the most important task that an entity can do. Through creativity an entity learns how to be responsible for the energies used in the creative process and to maximize the experiential opportunities that result from what has been created. Creativity and the experience associated with creativity is what existence is all about.

ME: *Creativity is a big subject to discuss and can lead us anywhere, but what I would like to understand is what area of creativity your entities specialize in and their intention in the learning and subsequent evolutionary opportunity presented to the entity who exists and works within Level 3.*

SE6: That is more than one question.

ME: Yes, it is isn't it?

SE6: O.K., let's work with it. Level 3 is in existence to provide the entity with all the necessary tools and energies to allow it to reach its maximum potential as a creative entity. Creativity though is not just about making objects or beings. It is about the creation of a framework or a road map in whatever form required to illustrate the possibilities for experience, growth and subsequent evolution of an entity as it approaches the point of opportunity. It is like a sign post along the way, saying, "Come here! Experience this! Evolve in this way!"

ME: So how do your entities do this?

SE6: They have the ability to inflate themselves dimensionally, creating their own inter-dimensionality whilst in a composite dimensional environment.

ME: And that is the way they create?

SE6: Absolutely. You see, they are in an environment that is constrained to a single composite dimension; it is limiting. The opportunity that presents itself here is for my entities to use their natural abilities to expand the environment presented to them in Level 3 by increasing the number of dimensions from one to as many as they want. This requires the entity to work with its peers on a most fundamental and personal level in a way that benefits all rather than the entity that is creating the opportunity for the new dimensional environment. The image you saw where the entities are within and without each other dimensionally illustrates this.

When an entity decides to enter into an agreement to work in this way with another entity, it opens up the possibilities for other entities to experience, create, and evolve in an alternative series of dimensions from that offered by Level 3 and the dimensions and environmental constructs offered by other partnerships.

ME: *I just saw an interesting image of clusters of entities working together in this way and then setting up an opportunity where the clusters of entities work with each other creating a multiple in excess of the sum of those dimensions already created by them as independent clusters. It's almost as if each cluster of ten individual entities created the opportunity for ten new dimensional environments, which could be in both the macro and micro scaling. Then adding them together does not create 10+10 dimensions but 10x10 dimensions—that's 100.*

SE6: Interesting, isn't it. A similar calculation is used to identify the useable dimensions available in your own environment, but those have been created for you by your Source Entity. In this example, the two clusters work through individual interactions of the entities, group interaction and intergroup interaction. Can you see the evolutionary opportunities presented here?

ME: *Let me see. One of the most important lessons I have learnt in my own environment is the ability to work together with someone or something without the need to get something in return—to give myself and/or my services gladly and freely whilst and when I can on a equal level with them, not in competition with them, sharing with them what I have and what I know so that they may learn, experience, and evolve. If this results in them evolving at a faster rate than me, then I will have been of true service. In doing this I work with people on a most intimate level, the level of full trust and acceptance. When I articulate the feeling I get when I work in this way, they want to experience it themselves. It's wonderful. This is what humanity should be doing— not trying to out-do each other. Being external to the competitive state is so liberating.*

SE6: Well done. Simply put, creating the opportunity to work together for the individual and collective good—that good being experience and evolution—is one of the most creative things an entity can achieve, which leads on to the fourth level. We are due to discuss Level 4 later.

Within each of the entities themselves is the ability to create whole universes within each of the dimensions that they create. They themselves are universal in volume, energy, and ability. This allows them unfathomable levels of creative opportunities, which in linking themselves together dimensionally magnifies the opportunity. The interdependencies required to create, sustain, and improve the environments created by these opportunities are far beyond the opportunities you have available to you. Even so, on a micro scale you have similar opportunities that are in keeping with how you have been created and the limitations of the environments you are designed to exist within. Part of the creativity process allows my entities to also create smaller environments and entities if they so wish. It is the level of responsibility required to maintain these entities and their environments whilst also working on their own level of interaction with their group members and intergroup members that permits them to grow and evolve as potential Source Entities in their own right.

ME: *Hold on a minute. Are you suggesting that your levels are a school for budding Source Entities?*

SE6: I would have thought that that was obvious from the size of them and what they can do.

ME: *Fine, but they are not able to be Source Entities outside of your environment, are they?*

SE6: Not currently, but they will.

My mind went back to the conversation with Source Entity Five and the ultimate plan of the Origin. All entities are destined to be free of their Source Entities and at this point every thing and every entity will ascend to a level of evolution above and beyond what is currently possible, even by the Origin. I wondered what will happen to these smaller Source Entities, the Source Entities of Source Entity Six.

SE6: Oh, they are destined to create the framework for the next level of evolution. You might want to chat to the Origin about it.

I thought further ahead to the work I will be doing after these dialogues, to the communications that will create "The Origin Speaks." That is going to be interesting. I mentally filed that thought and moved on to the next level in Source Entity Six's environment, Level 4.

Level 4—Learning Discrimination in the Creativity Process

ME: Let's move on to the next level then. In our previous dialogue on this subject, Level 4 is the recognition of creativity for evolutionary purposes. This looks a bit self-explanatory to me. Isn't being creative the route to certain evolution?

SE6: You would think so, but this is definitely not the case. Although creativity is one of the pre-requisites for evolutionary progression, it is also one that can result in a reduction in evolutionary progression if used incorrectly.

ME: I wasn't aware that at an energetic level creativity was anything else but educational and evolutionary.

SE6: Within the energetic level it is; however, within the physical realms that you inhabit, creativity can be used

242

for detrimental purposes. it can also be used incorrectly on the energetic levels, resulting in devolution. We will discuss this later. Right now I will advise you on the reasons for the creation of Level 4.

As I stated earlier, Level 4 is for the RECOGNITION of creativity for evolutionary purposes. It is the word "recognition" that I will focus on, as that is the reason for Level 4's existence. Any entity can create, and my entities are no exception to this rule, for creativity is one of the main functions given to us by the Origin. On Level 3 my entities learn about how to create and use creation for creating experiential opportunities. I described this in the last dialogue. What I have here is a level where the entity can experiment with the level and intention of its creativity to understand and recognize what creativity really is, and how it can affect its evolutionary opportunities and the entities that participate in their creations. As I said before, creativity is not only for creating what you would call positive evolution, it can also be used for negative evolution or devolution.

ME: *I thought devolution was pretty much impossible as everything we experience, whether we call it good or bad, results in our evolution.*

SE6: No, it's very much alive and well, especially in the lower energetic realms. Your own race experiences it on a regular basis. You call it karma.

ME: *But I thought that karma and evolution are mutually exclusive.*

SE6: They are, but karma should really be classified as evolution associated with that part of you that is experiencing the physical levels. It is relative only to your incarnate energies. It can also be called "minor evolution" with the "major evolution" being that which the whole of your energies, YOU, accrue.

ME: *Are you suggesting that evolution is split into separate parts—those parts being associated with those energies that are specific to a certain part of us that is experiencing existence in separation from the whole? That would mean that if we as energetic beings split off, say, twelve segments of our "selves" to experience existence and the various influences that the environments those existences have to offer, then we could potentially gain twelve separate packages of karma to deal with as part of our wholistic (referring to the "whole" of us) evolution. Each of those separate packages of karma may either add to or remove evolutionary progression, resulting in an average level of evolutionary progression.*

SE6: Correct. The opportunity presented to my entities in Level 4, therefore, is to be able to experiment in the creativity process and see what happens when so-called negative creativity is used in the creation process.

ME: *So what experiments do they perform to promote their recognition of the possibility that certain types of creativity can result in evolution vs. devolution?*

SE6: They create environments and entities without the use of their previous experience and the experience/common knowledge of their collective memory. Remember they can be in a position where they have already passed through this level before but may be re-experiencing it for "improvement of experience" purposes. In order for them to make the sort of creative mistakes that allow them to learn that certain types of evolution occur with certain types of creativity, they need to either enlist willing entities of their own evolutionary level or create a universal environment within their own energetic boundary to support a group of entities created specifically for the experiment in creativity. They then create that which they want to create and allow those entities who want to be involved in the experimental process to become exposed to the creation, whether it be an environment, entity, energy, or intention. If you also consider that involvement in such an experiment will only result in a "positive" level of evolution for those entities willing to participate (they are shielded from the possible effects of devolution even though they experience the devolutionary effects whilst the experiment is running), you reach a win-win condition where the creating entity can create what it likes and record the outcomes. The participating entities evolve in the process, irrespective of the evolutionary classification resulting from the outcome of the creativity experiment. The experiment's outcome is the recognition of the actions in the creativity process that can, could or will result in the evolution of the participating entities if they participate in the opportunities offered by that which has been created. Additional to this is the recognition of the actions in the creativity process that can, could, or will result in the devolution of the participating entities. In my environments, and I would expect in your own Source Entity's environments as well, creativity is an art that needs to be constantly refined to support the maximum evolutionary capability of what is being created, especially when an entity offers up the creation for use by its peers.

So in summary, Level 4 is used not only for the recognition of creativity for evolutionary purposes but for devolutionary purposes. The major lesson here is the discrimination of creativity processes to recognize and select only those that result in positive evolutionary opportunities even when the potential experience could be classified as negative to the entity experiencing the creation.

ME: *If it's that much of an art form to get it right how did you get it right?*

SE6: I didn't and I don't. This is the big issue with creativity. Ultimate levels of creativity can create ultimate levels of evolution or devolution. The trick is to understand the rules surrounding the creativity of creation that results only in positive evolutionary opportunities.

ME: *Hold on. Creativity is created?*

SE6: Yes, even creativity is created.

ME: *How is that done?*

SE6: With great care, thought, and consideration.

Me: *You are fooling with me.*

SE6: Not in the slightest. You see, an entity has to experience creativity before it is allowed to be a creator. Creativity is, therefore, created as a natural function of an entity's growth. More frequently though, it is a function manifested by the entity that is fully in control of the power it has and uses it with love and wisdom. Once an entity has mastered its power and uses it in love and wisdom, its creative function is switched on. It's a sort of coming of age.

Level 5—Evolutionary Experience Through Self-denial (A Prelude to Level 6)

ME: *Let's move on to the next and final level that you created—the level of evolutionary experience through self-denial, the ultimate sacrifice. This sounds a bit Christ-like to me.*

SE6: The reference is valid to a certain extent although in this instance it does not rely upon the ultimate sacrifice of self-destruction for the perpetuation of others.

ME: *I thought that was the ultimate sacrifice?*

SE6: It is, but it is not the basis for the function of this level of existence. If you were to observe the text you have just typed, you will notice that it is the use of "self-denial" to create the evolutionary experience and not "self-destruction."

ME: *Touché. I had better let you get on with the description of Level 5 then.*

SE6: That would be a good strategy.

ME: *Looking at the way your "universe"- sized entities exist and work, I would have thought that they pretty much fulfil the requirements of Level 5 by default?*

SE6: Not entirely. You see, whilst they are working within and without each other in the other levels, they are working towards their own evolution through the medium of experience in a normal and progressive way. In Level 5 the expectation is that they sacrifice their own evolution for the betterment of their peers.

ME: *How do they do this?*

SE6: By becoming an environment for the evolution of others. They do this without the prerequisite of needing to self-evolve as a result. They are available solely for the use and evolution of others. For a period (of time), they give up their own evolutionary plans and desires for evolution. They are being "of service" in a most fundamental way. Of course, they evolve as a result of such sacrifice, but they are unaware of this "evolutionary bonus" because I keep this from them. None of them realize that they benefit from being and working in Level 5. If they did, it would not serve its purpose.

ME: *How many entities are currently in Level 5?*

SE6: One.

ME: *One, only one?*

SE6: Yes, only one. There can only ever be one.

ME: *Why is that?*

SE6: Simply because Level 5 is created from that entity that wishes to work on Level 5.

ME: *What? Are you saying that, in actuality, Level 5 does not exist—that it's a virtual level?*

SE6: That is exactly what I am saying.

ME: *But that's a . . . conundrum!*

SE6: Let me explain further. To date I have only ever had one entity achieve Level 5.

ME: *And don't tell me—that entity is currently supporting the Level 5 environment.*

SE6: Correct. More importantly though, Level 5 is the level that supports the existence of all the other levels used for the experience and personal evolution of my entities.

ME: *This is starting to become very convoluted. Is everything about you and your entities convoluted?*

SE6: From your perspective you might say so, yes. From my perspective, it's not.

I had the impression that Source Entity Six was smiling. It was the sort of smile that a teacher has when the student finally starts to understand what is being conveyed. My understanding, though, would be very rudimentary and high level with no depth. I don't believe I could get any deeper into the mechanics of how all this was working. Everything about Source Entity Six appeared to be convoluted to the extreme with universal entities within and without each other creating environments for each other to exist and evolve within and without. Now I was being told that this within- and without-ness was continued by the creation of Level 5 as a function of an entity's desire to "give itself up" for the betterment of others by being an environment for ALL of them to exist within and without.

I could see it now; the entities could exist within each of the levels below Level 5 simultaneously. Their awareness of being in one of these levels for a second, third or more times was unlimited so that they are able to work out similar experiences with the opportunity to improve upon their actions and responses to situations they created or found themselves in. When one of them is evolved enough to progress to Level 5— i.e., they would not evolve any further by continuing to use the opportunities offered by Levels 1-4—and to date there has only ever been one entity to progress in its evolution to the point where it could be capable of being elevated to the Level 5 opportunity, it is advised by Source Entity Six that it does this for the evolution of its peers and that there is no benefit to itself. Its choice to progress to and become Level 5 is based upon pure selflessness. It is the mark of an entity that is capable of being a truly benevolent creator. One who expects nothing in return is a universally desirable trait and being prepared to arrest its own evolution for the betterment of others is true self-denial. Level 5 is not only the peak of evolution in Source Entity Six's environment, it is the environment where all the other levels exist within in all its composite dimensionality.

That was it! That was the reason for the composite dimensionality. (It had been bugging me for some time.) It was because the whole environment was created by that one entity that had attained enough evolution to allow it to be autonomous, to be Level 5. As a result, its dimensionality was constrained to what it was, a single universal entity stretched to its very limit to allow the existence of the other levels and the entities within it. Indeed, Level 5 was the ultimate sacrifice. In doing so, the entity was almost equal to Source Entity Six in stature.

SE6: Very well done. I was not sure that you would be expansive enough to understand.

ME: *I am flabbergasted, to say the least. I have to say that I didn't see that one coming.*

SE6: You almost missed it.

ME: *Yes, even now I am receiving images to help to understand further. The entity that has attained/elected to be Level 5 is expansive on an enormous scale. I get the impression that has had to swell itself to a size similar to you but within you. You are like two bubbles, one inside the other, with the outside skin of the inside bubble all but touching the inside skin of the outside bubble.*

SE6: Correct. There is very little volume left in me for my self, but that is my sacrifice. In effect, I am Level 6.

ME: No, no, don't confuse me.

SE6: I have to be the next level (six) in order to house the entity that is Level 5. It is logical.

ME: And you don't have any thing that is without? I know you have everything within.

SE6: The only thing that is without is the Origin. I might call it Level 7 . . . if you like?

ME: No, the Origin is fine.

SE6: Now you have my secret. You may go. You are released.

And Source Entity Six was gone. I sat at my computer with a head so full of images (to back up these few words of understanding) that I felt I was on a different level as well. I was fit to burst. I was stunned.

I sat at my computer and meditated for a moment. At this point I was half way through my dialogues with the children of the Origin, the Source Entities. Including our own Source Entity, I had been in contact with six to date. It had taken eighteen months. I have to admit to being more than a little tired. The energies used to both make and maintain the link with these entities were subtle and extremely high frequency, which for a low frequency (in comparison) entity such as myself, was demanding to maintain. The link never actually diminished though. As long as I needed to continue the dialogue, I was in some sort of contact with the Source Entity concerned, which included concurrent links with my own Source Entity. This I feel, was necessary as some of the channeled information and concepts often felt like they took a number of days to come down to my level and be translated within my brain into something that could be used in discussion. I was contemplating this further when my own Source Entity had a few words to say.

SE: You need to keep the ball rolling.
ME: *What do you mean?*
SE: Its time to get this information out into the public domain. You should continue these dialogues with a "Part Two" to this book, this one being "Part One."
ME: *Is that wise? Surely the information should stay together in one book?*
SE: It would be too big and too hard to read in one go. The information within this book needs to be available now because the time is right. Also, you need a break from the concentration of using energies that your physical body is not designed to be exposed to.
ME: *Would that explain why I am getting creaky joints that pop and bang all of a sudden? Or am I just getting old?*
SE: Your frequency level has been elevated as a result of these dialogues, but the speed of elevation has been rapid, not at the same speed as you would normally be experiencing, even with the ascension being as close as it is.
ME: *So how will I cope with the dialogues that I plan to have exclusively with the Origin?*

The Origin answered.

O: That will not be a problem, for you are linked to me via your Source Entity. I created your Source Entity, and your Source Entity created you. It is a clear lineage. When you communicate with the other Source Entities, you are not within the clear line of lineage and are energetically out of phase as a result. I believe this was explained to you in some way during the start of these dialogues.

I looked back at the manuscript; indeed, it was explained to me by my own Source Entity. I checked out the way I felt as I started my first dialogue with Source Entity Two. I felt like I was rubbing my head up and down the bark of an oak tree.

O: You will not experience any difficulty communicating with me. Indeed, have you ever experienced any difficulty in communicating with me once you established your method of rising up to the levels necessary to affect a clear unbroken link?

ME: *You're right. I haven't.*

O: Correct. Now you need to rest for a while and allow your energies to re-group, for the next six Source Entities will be more demanding than the last.

ME: *Now that's what I call encouragement.*

O: As you are aware, each of the Source Entities has its own resonant frequency. Your Source Entity has been working with you in the background to help maintain your connectivity and energy levels, and more importantly, your resilience. The first six were chosen for their closeness in frequency to your own Source Entity, each Source having a resonant frequency slightly further away than the previous one. The next six will be progressively further away.

ME: *I have just received an image of me being let out on a lead/rope, like a diver diving under ice.*

O: That is a good analogy. The further away you get from your home frequencies, the more alien the environment and the harder it is to get back—hence, the need for the rope being used to let you out slowly, Source Entity by Source Entity. When you finish the dialogues in the second book, you will be right out of your territory frequency-wise. You will truly have been where no man, of hu-man kind that is, has been before.

ME: I can't wait!

Afterword

To say this has been a difficult piece of work to channel would be an understatement (I believe I used the word "easy" somewhere, what a lie!), but I guess that's what gives it its validation. With *The History of God* I felt comfortable with the information that was being channeled through me. It had a homey feeling about it that was undoubtedly due to the fact that I was only dealing with entities within my Source Entity's multiversal environment and the associated frequencies. As the Origin explained to me in the final paragraphs of the last chapter, the creative energy/frequency lineage was pure. Dialogue with the Origin, the Source Entity, and me is, therefore, easier than the dialogues with the other Source Entities simply because they are of a differing energy/frequency lineage than I am. Had I been created by Source Entity Three, for instance, I would have had a harder time communicating with Source Entity One and an easier time communicating with Source Entity Three and so on. As a result, I am aware that the next series of dialogues with Source Entities Seven through Twelve will be progressively harder. In fact, I have been told it will be in the former text.

I feel though that I am up for the challenge and that the dialogues are a necessary part of awakening humankind's awareness of the possibility that beyond God (our Source Entity) is the very real greater reality that our God was, indeed, created by the greater God, the Absolute, the Origin.

I am fully aware that the information I received during these dialogues has not even scratched the surface of any of the Source Entities, their environments, or the creations that populate their environments, including our own. As a result, I fully welcome any additional information from other channeled sources that helps with both finding the individual

255

parts of the jigsaw that form the greater picture and putting them in the right place. As such, I now recognize that one of my major roles in this physicality is to help in some small way to assemble this picture and progress our collective knowledge, elevating us from this frequency we call the physical universe, returning us to our heritage of higher frequency, self-realized, all knowing, creative, and evolved existence.

I therefore give this message to the readers of this book.

If you believe deep down that these dialogues represent some part, no matter how small, of the greater reality, then you now know what I know and are opening the doors of awareness/self-realization and are, therefore, personally contributing to the effort to elevate the frequencies of Earth and its surrounding universe.

Your reading this book helps to do this.

For this I thank you.

Guy Steven Needler
16th March 2011

Glossary

Accurate "to boot" – An English way of saying an affirmative "as well"

Black Hole – A spiritual explanation is that a black hole is a small galaxy whose role is to collect lower frequency material into one place – within itself.

Cast-outs – Entities from Source Entity Two's environment that are ejected from a group association due to underperformance or the entity outgrowing the group.

Chela – The disciple of a religious teacher.

Cimension – A single dimension that has all the faculties of the first three lower dimensions we call up, down, left, right, forwards and backwards (3D), including other dimensions, without them needing to be singularly represented.

Coadunate – A collective state where a group of collectives are congregated together as a larger collective.

Fluidic Space – Space that is constantly changing in every way, from dimension to frequency.

Guru – A religious teacher or spiritual guide.

Hit the ground running – To start something new without the need to learn first.

Light Particle – A particle of light is known as a photon. A photon travels at the speed of 186,000 miles per second. The theoretical particle, the tachyon, is supposed to travel faster than the speed of light.

Loci/Locus – The center or source of an object/entity. Mathematically speaking, it is the set of all points or lines that satisfy a given requirement. In Source Entity Three's environment it represents the location of the majority of the entities concerned.

Magnetosphere – The outer region of a planet where the magnetic field of the planet controls the motion of certain charged particles.

Mahavatar – A divine incarnation. An entity that is incarnate with all memory of its energetic self, together with fully functioning energetic abilities.

Master – One who has mastered his/her subject matter.

Multipolous – A multiple of a multiple of a multiple. For instance X cubed, cubed, cubed ($X^{3,3,3}$).

Nova – A star that increases in brightness by many thousands of times its usual brightness, gradually fading to its original brightness. The last stages of the life of that star.

Pit Prop – A pole to reinforce the structure of a roof within a mine.

Pure of Heart – A lack of error in a creative condition.

SCUBA – An acronym for Self Contained Underwater Breathing Apparatus.

Self-realization – The function of being in full command of all our faculties as an energetic being whilst in the physical.

Spliced Undulation of Dimension - One or more dimensions linked together as a result of them being close together or overlapping in some part of their areas.

Stickle Brick – A child's building block similar to a Lego block but with spikes to join them together—like a Bristle Block.

Supernova - An exploding star caused by gravitational collapse.

The Big Bang – The current popular scientific explanation of how the universe started. The Source Entity stated in earlier dialogues with me that it was far from the truth—that it simply created our multiverse and, as such, it "winked" directly into existence. Whether this created a big bang is unclear from my dialogues.

The Grahoopnik – A race of entities that exist within the hearts of stars. Their existence depletes the stars' energies. Their leaving sometimes causes the star to go nova or supernova.

The speed of light – The speed of light is currently understood as being 186,000 miles per second.

Photograph by Anne Milner

About the Author

Guy Needler

Guy Needler MBA, MSc, CEng, MIET, MCMA initially trained as a mechanical engineer and quickly progressed on to be a chartered electrical and electronics engineer. However, throughout this earthly training he was always aware of the greater reality being around him, catching glimpses of the worlds of spirit. This resulted in a period from his teenage to early twenties where he revelled in the spiritual texts of the day and meditated intensively. Being subsequently told by his guides to focus on his earthly contribution for a period he scaled this back the intensity of spiritual work until his late thirties where he was re-awakened to his spiritual roles. The next six years saw him gaining his Reiki Master and a four year commitment to learn energy and vibrational therapy techniques from Helen Stott, a direct student of the *Barbara Brennan School of Healing*[TM], which also included a personal development undertaking (including psychotherapy) as a course prerequisite using the *Pathwork*[TM] methodology described by Susan Thesenga with further methodologies by Donovan Thesenga, John and Eva Pierrakos. His training and experience in energy based therapies have resulted in him being a member of the Complementary Medical Association (MCMA).

Along with his healing abilities his spiritual associations include being able to channel information from spirit including constant contact with other entities within our multiverse and his higher self and guides. It is the channelling that has resulted in *The History of God, Beyond the Source* and is producing further work.

As a method of grounding Guy practises and teaches Aikido. He is a 5th Dan National Coach with 30 years experience and is currently working on the use of spiritual energy within the physical side of the art.

Guy welcomes questions on the subject of spiritual physics and who and what God is.

Website: www.guystevenneedler.com

Email: beyondthesource@btinternet.com